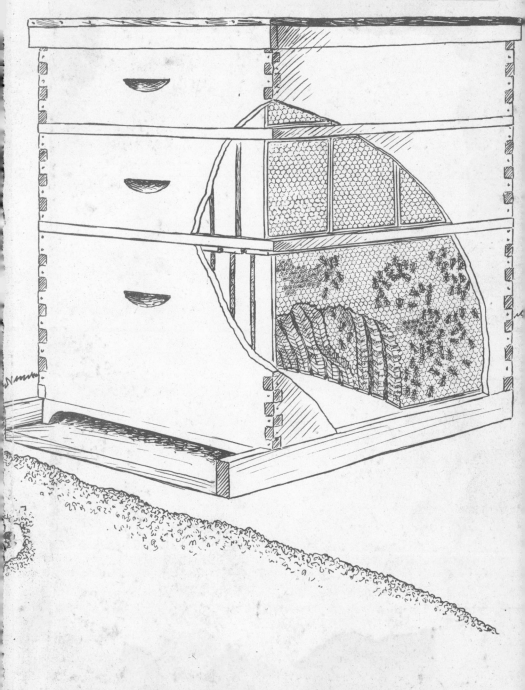

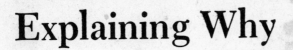

Explaining Why

By
Thomas I. Dowling
Kenneth Freeman
Nan Lacy
James S. Tippett

Illustrated by
Jean Busby
J. M. Swanson
C. E. B. Bernard

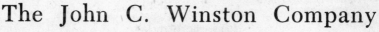

The John C. Winston Company

Chicago   Philadelphia   Toronto
Atlanta   Pasadena   Dallas

UNDERSTANDING SCIENCE

I Wonder Why

Seeing Why

Learning Why

Explaining Why

Discovering Why

Understanding Why

The authors wish to express appreciation to the teachers in the public schools of Lexington, Kentucky, for generous permission to use the materials that were mimeographed for their use.

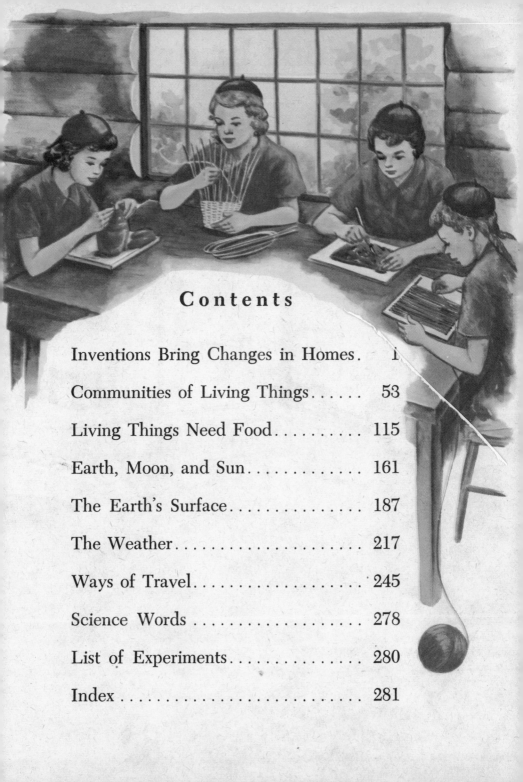

Contents

Inventions Bring Changes in Homes

The Modern House

"A modern house is being built near our home," Jane said to Miss Hall and the boys and girls in her classroom. "Its roof is different from any I have ever seen. Also, I have never seen so many windows in a house! Mother says she would not like the job of washing all that glass."

"Is it one of those modern houses you sometimes see in magazines?" Betty asked. "I like them. The windows let in plenty of fresh air and sunshine. There are pictures of some modern houses in a magazine we have here in our classroom."

1

"Modern houses are easy to keep clean, my mother says," Charles told the others while Betty was finding the magazine. "All the corners are rounded and dirt won't stick in them. The floors and walls are made of materials that are easy to keep clean. The rooms are arranged to save steps for the housekeeper. Mother says she thinks the men and women who plan modern houses know many science facts."

"This magazine has ten pictures of modern houses," Betty said. "I should like to live in any one of them."

"Oh," Jane said. "Here is a house almost like the one that is being built near our home. The roof has the same kind of slant. There are the same kinds of windows. Don't you think it looks different, Miss Hall?"

"I think I like it," Miss Hall said. "I have lived in the old home that my grandfather built. It was a modern house when it was built, but it was not well planned to save steps for housekeepers. Houses have been changed because people who lived in them wanted to be more comfortable. I suppose that everything in this modern house is planned to make living better and easier for those who live in it."

"Mother says the kitchens in modern houses are the kind she has always wanted," Susan said. "There are so many new inventions in them."

"Let's find out how inventions have made changes in homes," Dave said. "We can learn some more uses of science if we do."

2

Changes in Homes

Susan and Tom and the other boys and girls in Miss Hall's classroom made some trips to see different kinds of houses that people had built. They read about the homes of people in many lands.

Some houses are made of grass or logs. Not many inventions are needed to make a house of grass or logs. An axe or a knife would be needed and that is all, but an axe or a knife is made of steel. Steel is made from iron ore. Men had to learn how to take iron from the rocks of which it is a part. Then they had to learn how to change the iron ore into hard steel. They invented ways to do this because they needed tools like knives and axes.

If a house is made of boards, other tools than an axe and a knife are needed to shape the boards. Saws and planes are two of them. Hammers and nails are also needed to make a house of wooden boards. All these tools were made because men wanted to find better ways of doing their work or of making themselves comfortable.

3

Some houses are made of bricks. Some houses are made of cement, some are made of stone, and some are made of steel. Many other materials are used in new houses. Some of them are glass, rubber, cloth, and cork. Plastics are new materials that have been invented lately. Plastics are used in many ways. Inventors have been busy finding ways to use these materials for building houses.

Some houses have stairways. Most houses have chimneys of one kind or another. Some houses have few rooms and some have many rooms. Hinges, window shades, telephones, electric lights, furnaces, and screens for doors and windows are used in many houses. It is not easy to name all the materials and products of inventions that can be seen in houses.

Birds are not like human beings in building their homes. Birds of the same kind always build the same kind of nest. Anyone who has carefully observed a robin's nest will be able to say that another nest is or is not a robin's nest. The nest may be on a flat board under a protecting roof or in a tree, but it will be made in the same way if it is a robin's nest. No one who knows a hummingbird's nest will say that it is the nest of any other bird. These are pictures of the nests of birds.

Robin   Hummingbird   Oriole

Insects of the same kind always make the same kind of home. The paper wasp does not make a nest or home like the home of a mud dauber or of a hornet. They are different kinds of insects, and they make different kinds of homes. Anyone who has observed a hornet's nest will never say that it is a paper wasp's nest. These are pictures of their homes.

Paper wasp   Mud dauber   Hornet

The home that a rabbit makes for its young ones is not like the nest that a squirrel makes for its young. Many animals do not make homes for their young ones, but an animal that does make a nest or home always makes the same kind of home in the same way. Different materials may be used. The nest or home may be in a different kind of place, but it is always made in the same way.

5

Human beings do not make the same kinds of homes that they did in the early times. The homes change because people invent ways of making them better. Ways of living change and homes are made to meet these changing needs. These are some of the kinds of homes that people have made.

Old and New Ways of Lighting Houses

"I am making a page in my Notebook for Science to show a simple home of early days in America," Jane said. "It is a house like the one we saw on our trip."

Jane showed the pictures that she was putting in her notebook. One picture was of an open fireplace. Near the fireplace there were many pans and kettles that the people used for cooking. Some of the pans had long handles so that they could be held over the fire. There was an iron rod over the fire where kettles and pots could be hung. Another picture showed the kind of lamps people used.

"I suppose at first people used the light from a fireplace to light the room," Jane said. "Then they put oil in a flat pan. They laid a piece of string in the oil and let it fall over the edge of the pan. The string could be lighted, and the lamp could be taken from one part of the room to another."

"Some people in early times set fire to pieces of wood and read by the light," Dave said.

"The candle was a real invention," Betty said. "A candle is a piece of string in wax. We use candles sometimes at my home now."

"I know how to make candles by dipping a thick string in hot melted wax," one of the other children said. "We made them last year for Christmas gifts. I will show you how to make candles someday. They are not hard to make."

"I have a picture of a candle mold in my book," Jane said. "The string is the wick. You can see how each wick was run through one of the parts of the candle mold. It was fastened at each end. Then melted tallow was poured into the open end of the mold. Tallow is the fat from animals such as cows and sheep. It gets solid when it is cool. When the tallow in the candle mold was cold, the whole mold was dipped in hot water and then the candles were lifted out of the molds."

"I saw a candle mold in the old house we went to see," Sam said. "It was just like your picture, Jane."

After they had all looked at the candle mold, Jane showed other pictures that she had pasted in her Notebook for Science. "Oil from whales was used in lamps like this," she said. "They were called whale-oil lamps."

"I see that you have a picture of a kerosene lamp," Sam said.

"I have put pictures of many kinds of lamps in my notebook," Jane said. "You can see that I have lamps that burn gas and lamps that use electricity for making light. New inventions are being made all the time to make lighting better."

8

Some Experiments in Lighting

1. Making Candles in Molds

Bring some fat that comes from cows or sheep. You should bring two or three pounds of it. The fat from the sheep or cow will have other materials in it. Only pure tallow is used in making tallow candles. How can you get pure tallow from the fat you bring? Try it this way.

Pour two cups of water into a pot or pan. Put the fat in the pan with the water. Set the pan over an electric hot plate or some other source of heat. Let the fat and water boil until the fat has melted and become liquid. Then take the pan from the heat, and let the mixture cool. The tallow will be a hard yellow material over the top of the cooled mixture. Lift it off after it is hard. What is left in the pan?

Now clean the pan, and put the pure tallow back into it. Put the pan with the tallow in it over the heat. The tallow will melt.

Wicks for candles are made from loosely twisted cotton or linen threads. Make wicks and dip them into hot tallow. The wicks will be stiff when the tallow cools. Make the wicks straight. Then you can hang the wicks in test tubes.

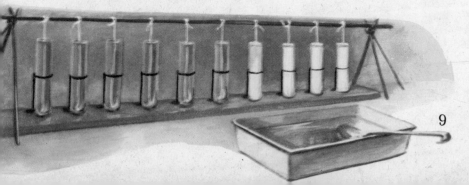

9

Pour the hot tallow into glass test tubes with the wicks in them. Test tubes are used in place of a candle mold because candle molds are hard to find. Set the test tubes aside to cool. You can dip the tubes into cold water to make the tallow harden more quickly. When you are sure that the tallow is hard, dip the test tube into a pan of hot water. Do it quickly. Why must you do it quickly? You can explain why if you let one test tube with tallow in it stay in hot water for a few minutes. As soon as you take the tube from the hot water, pull the candle from the tube. Why does the candle come easily from the tube? Light one of the candles to prove that you have done your work carefully.

Other materials can be used in place of the tallow from cows or sheep. Paraffin is a good material to use. Paraffin is a material that usually comes from petroleum when it is heated. A white wax from the honeycomb of bees can be used. Whale oil is a good material to use.

If you make a candle of whale oil seven-eighths of an inch across and light it, you will have one candle power of light. Light is measured by candle power. What does ten candle power mean?

2. How an Oil Lamp Burns

This is an oil lamp. It has a clear glass chimney. The bowl is made of glass. Oil is put into the bowl. Then a flat wick of cotton or linen is put in a holder. The holder is fastened on the bowl so that one end of the wick is in the oil. Look at the holder. It is an interesting invention. There is a little wheel that is used to turn the wick up or down. The chimney fits into the holder and is held there. Why are holes put in the flat part of the holder? Does heat rise from the top of the chimney when the wick is lighted? What comes in through the holes in the flat part of the holder? If you covered all the holes in the flat part of the holder, what would happen to the burning wick?

Kerosene is the oil that is used in this kind of lamp. Kerosene comes from coal or petroleum. Petroleum is oil that is found in the earth. Oil wells are made, and petroleum is pumped from oil wells. Sometimes it flows out naturally from the well.

Gas is used sometimes for lighting and heating houses. Dave and the others learned about gas when they studied about heating homes.

11

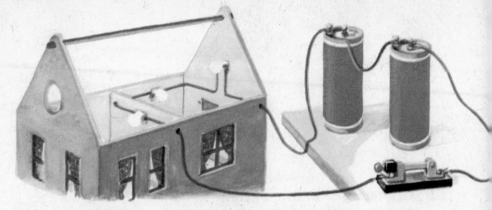

3. Lighting a Doll House

Today most houses are lighted by electricity. This is a doll house that Jane and Sam made. It shows how a house is lighted by electricity. Two lines of covered copper wire are run from two dry cells. Wires that are covered well are said to be insulated. Electricity in a wire that is not insulated may cause a fire. The picture shows how to run the wires. Electricity is made in the dry cells. It flows through the wires from the dry cells where it is made. The wires form a path or circuit for the electricity.

Small light sockets are joined by other insulated wires to the lines of wire from the dry cells. A simple electric light switch is placed on one of the wires from the dry cells. Small flashlight bulbs are fitted into the sockets. When the switch is closed, the lights will come on all over the house. Could you put a switch in a wire to each of the lights and turn off that light without turning off the other lights? You could perform some experiments with only one or two lights before you wire the doll house for electricity.

Changes in Heating Homes

Anyone who has stood in sunshine and then moved into shade knows that sunshine is warm. The sun gives heat. Many animals need some sunshine for growing. Even lizards and snakes, that are cold-blooded animals, come out on the first warm days of spring into the sunshine. It is easy to observe animals lying in warm sunshine.

Human beings need and enjoy sunshine. They like to be warm. They have invented ways to make cloth for clothes to help keep themselves warm. They have invented ways to keep their houses warm.

The boys and girls and Miss Hall made charts to show all the changes that have been made in heating.

The first way to heat a home was an open fire built on the ground. Someone found out how to make a fire by striking two hard rocks together or by rubbing two pieces of wood together. Striking rocks together or rubbing pieces of wood or other materials together causes friction. Friction makes heat. From the heat of friction, a fire could be made to burn. The sticks were laid on so that air could get to the fire to keep it burning. People would get near to the burning fire to keep warm.

If an open fire is built in a cave or a tent, smoke will rise from it. Why does smoke rise? The first invention to improve heating a home in a cave or tent was to cut a hole in the roof. What would that do to make heating better?

The next invention was a fireplace. To build a fire-place, rocks were laid around the place where the open fire would be. A chimney with a hole through it was built to the roof so that smoke could get outside. Much of the heat from the fire went up the chimney, too. Why did it do that?

The open fireplace gave heat for the house. Cooking could be done over it. Even today some houses have only open fireplaces for heat. Many houses have fireplaces for enjoyment and for heat even though much of the heat still goes up the chimney.

Then people found out something more about heat. Some materials keep their heat longer than others. Rock is a material. Brick is a material. Iron and steel are materials. Glass, wood, and human bodies are materials. Fireplaces are usually built of rocks or bricks. When rocks and bricks are heated in a fire, they stay hot for a long time. Sometimes ovens are made of bricks or rocks. If a fire is made inside the oven, the bricks or rocks will stay warm long after the fire has stopped burning. How could people use that fact of science?

In early days, before cars with heaters in them had been thought of, people used to wrap a hot brick or rock in cloth. They put it on the floor of the carriage or wagon before they made a trip in cold weather. The wrapped brick stayed warm for a long time. It made a good foot warmer. Hot water is sometimes put in a rubber bottle that is wrapped in cloth and used for a warmer.

Then stoves were invented. The Franklin stove was one of the first stoves that was invented. Observe how much like a fireplace it is. Why would it be made like a fireplace?

There are other kinds of stoves on the next page. One of them is a cook stove. It has an oven and there are lids on top. The lids can be lifted off so that pots and pans can be put nearer to the fire. In one of the lids on top of the stove is a lifter for taking the lid off. Why does the lifter have a special kind of handle?

Betty and Dave and the other boys and girls in Miss Hall's classroom know that heat travels faster in some materials than in others. It is easy to perform an experiment to show it.

An Experiment with Heat

Get an iron rod and put a wooden handle on one end. Get another iron rod of the same length and size, but do not put a handle on it. Hold one rod in each hand. Put the other ends of the rods in heat. Which rod can you hold longer? You may use other materials for the experiment. The lifter for the lid on the cook stove has a handle of wire. Could you hold it longer than you could hold a lifter with a solid iron handle? Why?

15

After stoves were invented, people began to use different kinds of fuels to burn for heat. First of all, wood was burned for fuel in most places. That was because wood was easy to get. Trees or woody plants grew in most places on the earth.

Coal is another kind of fuel that is used for making heat. Coal is found in the earth. It is not found in all places in the earth. Coal is sometimes burned in an open fireplace. Special stoves were made for burning coal.

This is the picture of a coal mine. Men are mining the coal from deep in the earth and bringing it up for use in making heat for homes and schools and for use in many other ways. Sometimes coal is found near the top of the ground. Then it is mined easily.

Oil is another kind of fuel. It comes from deep in the earth. Special kinds of stoves had to be invented for burning oil. Furnaces in many homes burn oil for making heat. Oil is placed in tanks outside or in the house. It goes through a small pipe to the furnace room and into the heater where it is burned.

17

Oil is used as a fuel to make heat for cooking, for heating a room, or for heating a small stove that can be moved from one room to another. These are pictures of a cookstove that is heated by the burning of oil, of a space heater that uses oil for fuel, and of a small oil stove.

Gas is another fuel that is used for making heat. Gas for fuel sometimes comes from the earth. This is called natural gas. In some places on the earth, natural gas is pouring from a crack in the earth. If it is lighted, it burns.

Gas for fuel is sometimes made by turning coal or other materials into gas. This is called artificial gas. Natural gas is made by nature. Artificial gas is made by man. When changes in ways of living made it desirable to have more gas than nature had produced, men invented ways to make artificial gas.

Artificial gas to burn as fuel for heat and for light is often made in city gas plants. The gas is kept in huge round tanks.

18

Natural gas or artificial gas is sometimes burned in fireplaces. It is burned in stoves and in furnaces, too. Gas was once used for light in many houses. Gas can be bought in tanks and taken home for burning. Gas comes to the stove or the light through an iron or copper tube. A handle on a stopper at the end of the tube is turned to let the gas come out or to stop it from coming out. If a lighted match is held to the gas when it comes out, the gas burns. Gas can be as dangerous as fire, but gas is more dangerous than wood, coal, or oil. Gas is dangerous to breathe. It cannot be seen. People who use it learn to be careful. They never leave the stopper to the tube open unless the gas is being burned.

The objects in this picture are used in connection with the burning of gas. Tell about the purpose and use of each object.

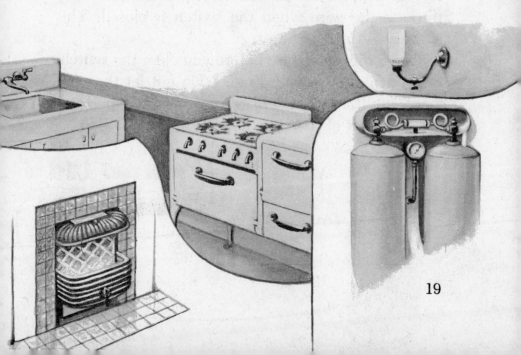

Electricity for Heat and Light

As ways of living changed, wood, coal, and gas were not producing all the heat and light of the kind that men wanted. A new way was found to produce both heat and light with electricity.

Electricity is not a fuel, but it produces heat and light. The use of electricity in homes has made it possible to improve living in many ways. Television, radio, telephones, electric lights, and electric motors all use electricity in some way.

An Experiment with Electricity

Does electricity make heat? You can easily find out. Take a dry cell, an electric switch, and some small wire that is not insulated. Fasten the wire to the dry cell and the electric switch to make a circuit. It will be possible for an electric current to run through the wire when the switch is closed. This is the way to do it.

Touch the small wire before you close the switch. Is it warmer than your finger? Do not let the wire touch anything that will burn when you perform the next part of the experiment.

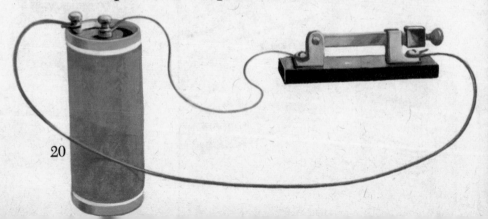

Close the switch. Touch the small wire. What happens to the wire if you leave the switch closed for a short time? Why is a wire that carries an electric current covered or insulated? Look at a burner on an electric hot plate or stove. When the switch is turned so that a current runs through the burner, what happens to the burner?

The electricity that is used for lights and for heat in homes is made in electric plants. It is sent over wires into houses. An electric switch turns the current on or off. Sometimes the switch has ON and OFF printed on it so that the user can tell when the current is on or off. In what other way can the user tell when the current is coming over the wires into a light bulb or into an electric stove?

One dry cell makes only a small current of electricity to send over wires. An electric plant makes a large current. Dry cells usually are not used for heating or for making lights. It takes a large electric current to heat the wires in an electric stove or in any of these inventions that can be found in many homes.

21

Inventions for Using Electricity

Scientists found out some of the facts about electricity. It could be used for heat. It could be used for light. It could be made in electric plants. Then inventors began to work. They invented all kinds of things that use electric current. They invented ways to make the use of electricity safe.

One important invention is the electric fuse. Electricity can be dangerous. It can set fire to materials if the wire that carries it becomes too hot. The electric fuse is an invention to cut off the electric current when there is too much electricity flowing over the wire.

Making a Simple Fuse

Get two paper clips. Bend one end of each paper clip so as to form a foot. (See picture 1.)

Get two short pieces of insulated wire. Scrape the insulation from each end of the wire. Place a small tack through the foot of the paper clip. Make a loop in one end of the scraped wire, and nail the tack through the loop on to a block of wood. (See picture 2.)

Cut some pieces of tinfoil from a wrapper. Cut them in the shape that you see in picture 3. One of these pieces of tinfoil is fastened between the two paper clips. (See picture 4.)

This is a simple fuse. See the next page for showing how the fuse works.

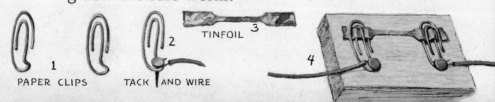

1   PAPER CLIPS   TACK AND WIRE   2   TINFOIL 3   4

How a Simple Fuse Works

You will need two dry cells, an electric switch, some insulated wire, a flashlight bulb and a light socket, and the simple fuse you have made. Connect them as the picture shows.

Now scrape the insulation from two places on the wires that are connected to the light socket. Be sure that these two places are not touching each other, or touching anything that will burn. Close the electric switch. The flashlight bulb lights up.

Now touch the two bare places on the wires together as the second picture shows. The tinfoil fuse gets hot and melts. The flashlight bulb goes out.

Why did the fuse burn out? The touching of the two bare wires caused a short circuit. Electricity always flows through the shortest path it can. More of it flows through the tinfoil when the path is made shorter. This causes the tinfoil to melt and to break the flow of the current. The insulated wire would become very hot if the fuse did not melt first. If wires became too hot, a fire might be started. That is why we have fuses in all electric currents. When the cause of the short circuit is corrected, a new fuse may be put in and the current will flow again.

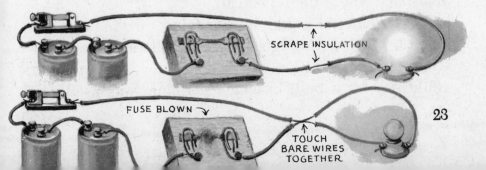

SCRAPE INSULATION

FUSE BLOWN

TOUCH BARE WIRES TOGETHER

Thomas A. Edison, Scientist and Inventor

Thomas Alva Edison was born in Ohio a little more than one hundred years ago. He was always asking questions. If anyone could not answer his question, he would ask, "Why can't you answer?"

When he was still a young boy, he got a job selling papers on a train. He fitted up a workshop in a part of the small corner he was allowed to use in the train. He was always performing experiments. In a few years he got a job as a telegraph operator. Then his real work as a scientist and an inventor began.

He sold one of his inventions to make telegraphing easier. He sold it for forty thousand dollars. With that money he set up a science laboratory in New Jersey. Then he began work to make an electric light that anyone could buy and that would be better than any light then known. He filled two hundred notebooks with ideas that he had for experiments and with results of experiments he and his helpers tried. At last, after less than a year of experimenting, Edison decided that the light he wanted would burn in a glass bulb from which all the air had been pumped. When all the air was pumped out of the bulb, a vacuum was made inside the bulb. A vacuum is a space where there is no air.

What material could be used for carrying the electric current through the bulb? Platinum was tried. It burned with a white light, but few people could pay for a bulb in which platinum was used.

Then Edison tried a plain thread of cotton which he had prepared in a special way. It was hard to put the thread in the glass bulb from which all air had been pumped and where a vacuum had been made. It was hard to keep any part of the thread from touching any other part, but at last everything was ready. The electric current was connected. The thread inside the bulb glowed red and then it grew white with heat in the vacuum. Edison and his helpers watched. The light burned for one hour, two hours, ten hours, thirty hours, and forty hours before the prepared cotton thread burned out. The experiment was a success. Edison and his helpers had given to the world a new kind of light. It was the kind of electric light that almost everyone uses now. Many more experiments were necessary before the electric light was what Edison wanted it to be. Experiments showed ways to make the light burn longer. No invention that Thomas Alva Edison ever made in his lifetime as a scientist and an inventor has helped human beings more than the electric light.

Take an old electric light bulb and see how it is made. Be careful! Broken glass can cut you! How is the wire that carries the current inside the bulb kept from touching itself at any place? What would happen if it did touch itself?

Running Water in Homes

All living things need water. At first human beings needed water only to drink. Drinking water was needed to keep them alive. Swimming may have been natural to them, too. After a while human beings began to use water for other purposes than drinking and swimming. When human beings had been in the world long enough, they began to want to clean their hands and faces and other parts of their bodies. Water was near by, and someone used it for washing hands and then for taking a bath. After clothes were made, water was used to keep them clean. It was used in cooking, too.

The homes of human beings have always been placed where water could be found. Sometimes the house was built near a river or near the shore of a lake. Sometimes it was built near a spring. A spring is a place where water flows from the earth. Water seeps down into the earth after a rain or snow. It may seep into the ground from rivers or lakes. Under the ground, the water may run together into larger streams just as it does on top of the ground. If an underground stream flowed down from hills and mountains, it might run out of the ground. Some springs are large streams. Most of them are small trickles of water. If the house could not be built close to the spring or stream, water was carried to the house by hand. Carrying water from a spring to the house is not an easy job.

If anyone had to carry water from a spring to a house, he would try to think of ways to make it easier to get water into the house. Could a hole be dug in the ground to hold water that might run from the roof of the house when it rained? Could a hole be dug in the ground near the house to reach a stream that was flowing underground? They could both be done. Wells were dug and lined with stones or bricks. A top was placed over them. Troughs were made to take the water from the roof of the house to the well. If rains came often enough, the well had water in it for drinking and for other purposes. If the spring that was underground did not stop running, the well that held spring water had water in it for all needs. Wells that were built near the house made living better for the people in the house.

If anyone had a well with water in it near his house, he would need to get the water from the well into his house. How could he do it?

He could tie a rope to a bucket and draw water from the well and carry the bucket of water into the house. This boy is getting water that way.

27

Someone thought of this way to get water from a well. He used a large wheel with a crank for a handle. The large wheel with the crank for a handle is a wheel and axle. It is a machine for making work easier. The longer the handle of the crank, the easier it is to lift the bucket of water. All these ways use simple machines to make drawing water from a well easier. One uses a pulley. One uses a lever. Pulleys and levers are simple machines just as a wheel and axle is a simple machine.

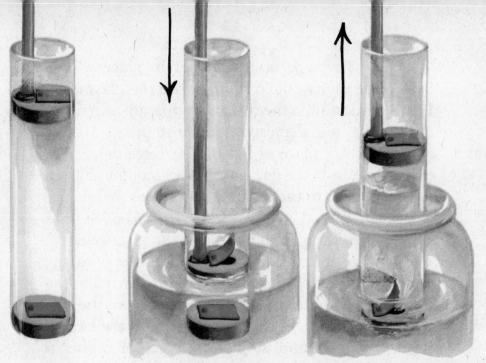

A Simple Pump

Then someone invented a pump. This is the way to make a simple pump.

Get a glass tube, such as a straight lamp chimney. Get a two-hole rubber stopper that fits closely inside the tube and a one-hole rubber stopper which fits into the end of the glass tube. Get a smooth round stick a little longer than the glass tube.

Push the stick through one hole of the two-hole rubber stopper. Place a rubber band or string above and below the stopper on the stick to keep the stopper from slipping off. Cut a piece of rubber from an old balloon, or bicycle inner tube, large enough to cover the other hole of the two-hole rubber stopper.

Fasten the piece of flat rubber in place with a tack. Slide the two-hole stopper into the glass tube. If it is hard to slide the rubber stopper up and down in the tube, put some soap on the stopper.

Cut another piece of flat rubber large enough to cover the hole in the one-hole rubber stopper. Fasten the flat rubber to the stopper with a tack. When the stopper is placed in the end of the tube, the flat rubber should be on the inside of the glass tube.

Place the glass tube in a jar of water with the closed end under the water. Push down on the handle. Watch the flat rubber piece on the top stopper. Air pushes past the top piece as the handle is pushed down and the bottom piece of rubber is closed. When the handle is pulled up, the top piece is closed and the bottom piece opens. Water enters the tube. Now as the handle is pushed up and down, water will rise in the tube.

It is the pressure of the air that forces the water up into the tube. As air is forced from the tube, air pushes the water into the space in the tube. The pieces of rubber are like doors, but they let the water flow in only one direction.

Air Presses against Everything

The simple pump that you can make uses the force of air to push the water up a pipe or tube. These experiments will help you understand that air is all around in space and that it presses against everything.

1. Air Fills Up Space

You will need a bottle and a one-hole rubber stopper. Push the stem of a small glass funnel through the hole of the stopper. Then fit the stopper into the bottle. Pour water into the funnel. Before any water enters the bottle, a bubble of air must leave the bottle through the water. Water runs into the bottle in spurts.

Put a bottle with a narrow neck into a pan of water. Lay the bottle on its side. A gurgling sound is produced as the air leaves and the water enters the bottle.

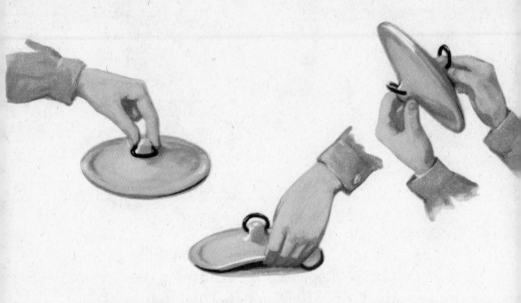

2. Sticking Sink Stoppers

Get a flat rubber sink stopper which has a knob in the center. Moisten the stopper with water and press it against a smooth surface. A table top will do for the smooth surface.

Then try to lift the stopper by the knob. When the moistened stopper is pressed against the table top, all the air under it is pressed out. The push of the air on top of the stopper holds it in place.

Now try lifting the stopper by pulling up the edge of the stopper. It comes up easily when air is allowed to get under it. The pressure or push of the air is the same on both sides of the stopper.

Moisten two flat sink stoppers and press them together. Try to pull them apart by the knobs. Is it hard or easy to do this?

3. A Rubber Force Cup

Get a rubber force cup which is used to open sinks when they have become stopped. Moisten the rubber part with water and press it upon a smooth surface such as a table top.

Then try to pull it up by the handle. A great force is needed to pull it up.

The push of the air holds the rubber cup to the table. As you pressed against the cup, some of the air under it was pushed out. When you lift the rubber cup, you must lift the air that is pressing down on it.

4. Hanging a Coat on Air

Get a coat hanger which has a rubber cup for fastening it to a wall. Usually the rubber cup has to be moistened with water before pressing it to the wall.

Pressing the rubber cup against the wall removes the air from under the cup. The push of the air on the outside of the cup holds it in place.

This kind of coat hanger will hold up an overcoat.

← Rubber cup

← Steel hook

33

5. Crushing a Can

Get a used gallon can and a solid rubber stopper. First, place a board on the can and have several people stand upon it. The can is strong.

Then pour about one teacup of water into the can and heat the water to boiling. Remove the can from the fire and place the rubber stopper in the mouth of the can. Let the can cool.

The push of the air from the outside will crush the can. The push of the air outside the can was the same as the push of air inside until the air was pushed from the inside of the can by the steam.

6. Filling a Balloon in a Flask

A glass flask and a rubber balloon are needed. Put enough water into the flask to cover the bottom of the flask to a depth of one-half inch. Heat the flask until the water boils. Take the flask from the fire and quickly pull the opening of the balloon over the mouth of flask. Let the flask cool.

The balloon is forced into the flask by the push of the air on it.

In these experiments Miss Hall's class learned that air presses against everything. Are there other facts of science that they learned? You could make a list of them for your Notebook for Science.

Water for Homes in Cities

When homes were built close together in towns and cities, springs and wells and pumps were not enough to furnish a supply of water for all the homes. Other ways of bringing water into homes were found. Water was pumped by engines into a water tank on a high hill in a small city. Then the water was taken into the homes through pipes. This is a drawing to show how it was done.

Sometimes water was brought to the city from a lake on a high hill far from the city. The lake was sometimes one that nature had made. Sometimes it was a lake, or reservoir, that men had made.

This is a supply of water that has been made by damming up a stream. This water is used by the people in the city near by. In this picture water is being brought from the lake by a large pipe. What makes the water flow through the pipe? Why do you suppose the lake, or reservoir, is on high ground?

The large pipe is called an aqueduct. The water runs from the reservoir through the aqueduct to the power house, or pumping station. Engines in the power house pump the water through another large pipe to the city.

After water is brought into the city by the large pipe, it is taken to the homes by smaller pipes.

This is a drawing to show how the stream of water in the large pipe is divided into smaller streams to supply all the homes in the city.

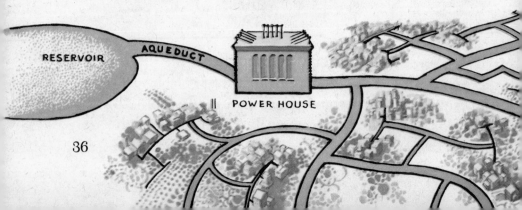

RESERVOIR

AQUEDUCT

POWER HOUSE

A Bathroom

This is a bathroom in a city home. Observe everything in it. Inventors have been at work planning for all these ways to help people keep themselves clean. You can probably answer these questions about the bathroom in your home.

1. Does the water come from a tank or a lake?
2. How is the water for the bathroom heated?
3. Where does the waste water go?
4. How do you get water of the right temperature for washing your face and hands or for bathing?

More about Water Pressure

In every bathroom something causes water to come through the pipes. You know that water runs downhill. If a lake were placed on a high hill, the water would come through the pipes with greater force.

This experiment shows that water presses upon the water below it. If the supply of water were placed on a low hill, would the water come into the bathroom with much force?

An Experiment with Water Pressure

For this experiment you will need a gallon can. Punch a hole with a nail near the bottom of the can. Punch another hole halfway between the top and bottom. Punch a third hole near the top of the can.

Cut small wooden pegs to fit the holes. Place the can over a sink and fill the can with water. Take out the pegs. The distance the water is forced away from the can is not the same for each hole. Each hole has different amounts of water over it. You may keep filling the can as the water flows out. Can you explain from this experiment why dams are built with very thick bottoms while the tops of the dams are very narrow? Is the pressure of water greater on the bottom of the dam?

An Experiment to Explain a Fountain

You can learn more about water pressure by performing this experiment.

Cut the bottom out of a gallon can. Get a one-hole rubber stopper that will fit the mouth of the can. A cork stopper with a hole in it will do. Put a short piece of glass tubing into the hole of the stopper. Fasten a long piece of rubber tubing onto the glass tubing. Use a rubber band to hold it in place. In the other end of the rubber tubing, place the glass part from a medicine dropper. Place the medicine dropper through the hole in the bottom of a flower pot. The glass part should almost reach the top of the pot. Fill the pot with sand or small pebbles to the top of the glass. Place the pot on two bricks in a pan. Turn the gallon can upside down, and fill it with water. Put the gallon can on a high shelf or table.

Raise the pan to see what happens to the fountain. Use a clothespin to stop the flow of water.

If water is pressed upon by air that has been compressed or made to fit into a smaller space, it will come into the bathroom or kitchen with greater force. Air can be compressed in many ways. This is one way to do it and to make it force water through a small pipe.

A Compressed Air Fountain

Get a two-hole rubber stopper that fits a milk bottle. Put the glass part of a medicine dropper through one hole of the rubber stopper. The end should point out of the bottle. Fasten a piece of rubber tubing to the medicine dropper. The tubing should reach to the bottom of the bottle.

Place a short piece of glass tubing in the other hole of the rubber stopper. Put a piece of rubber tubing onto the glass tube. Fill the milk bottle with water. Blow into the rubber tube.

The pressure of the air pushes the water through the medicine dropper.

You may wish to put a bicycle pump onto the rubber tube and compress the air in that way.

40

"I think the important thing about the use of water in homes is that it does not have to be carried from a spring or a well," Tom said. "I went to camp this summer and we had to carry water from a spring that was at the foot of a hill. They are going to put a force pump near the spring next year and push the water into the tank on a hill above the camp."

"We sometimes go to a house in the country near us where they get water that way," Susan said. "A pipe runs from the pump in the basement of the house to a deep well a little way downhill from the house. Electricity is used to run the pump. Water is pumped from the well into a tank near the pump. The tank is closed at the top. When water is pumped into the tank, the air in the tank is compressed or forced into a smaller space. Pipes take the water from the tank to all the bathrooms and to the kitchen in the house."

"I can draw a picture to show just how it works," Sam said, and he did it quickly.

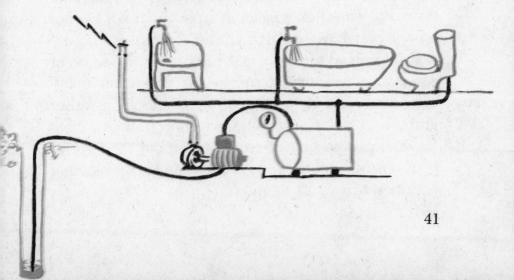

"I would not know how to invent a force pump, a tank, or an electric motor to run the pump," Susan said. "I can understand Sam's drawing. I know about compressed air, for I compress air into my bicycle tire every time I pump it up. You can feel the force of compressed air if you take the cap from a bicycle tire and let out air."

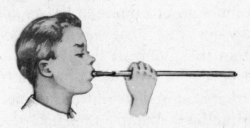

Making a Compressed Air Gun

This is an experiment to show that compressed air has force.

Get a glass tube about two feet long or longer. Put a matchstick in it and push the stick down toward the end of the tube into which you are to blow. Be sure the stick moves easily. Blow hard into the tube. The stick will shoot from the tube. Do not blow toward anyone! It may be dangerous.

Compressed air has great force. It is the force of compressed air which forces the shot from many "air" guns, and they are just as dangerous as other guns. It is safest not to have a gun.

Some people that do not know about modern inventions use "blow" guns to kill animals by blowing poisoned arrows at them.

Using Science to Make Better Homes and Schools

One morning Sam showed the others in the classroom a chart that Tom and Susan and he had made. This is their chart.

HOW FACTS OF SCIENCE ARE USED TO MAKE BETTER HOMES

1. Facts about Heat
   a. Heat travels faster in some materials than in others.
   b. Heated air rises.
   c. Heated water rises.
   d. Heat stays longer in some materials than in others.
   e. Friction causes heat.
   f. Burning fuel makes heat.
   g. An electric current makes heat.
   h. The sun gives heat.

2. Facts about Light
   a. Light travels in straight lines.
   b. Light can be reflected.
   c. Surfaces that are lighter in color reflect more light.
   d. Burning makes light.
   e. An electric current makes light.
   f. The sun gives light.

3. Facts about Water
   a. Water has force.
   b. Human beings need water for drinking.
   c. Water helps keep things clean.
   d. Water runs from higher to lower places.
   e. Air can be compressed to force water uphill.
   f. Sometimes water flows underground.

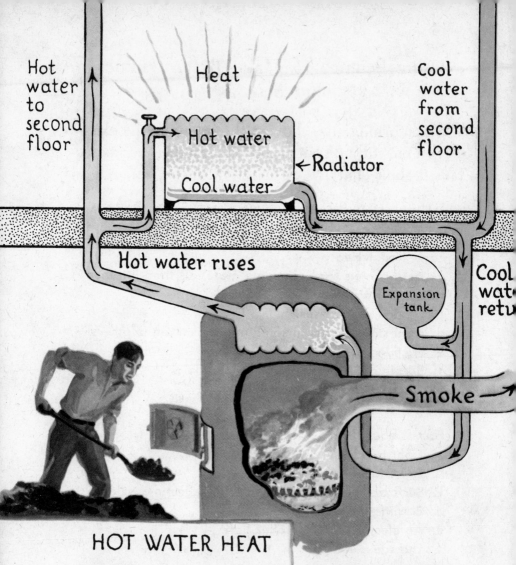

Hot water to second floor

Heat

Cool water from second floor

Hot water

← Radiator

Cool water

Hot water rises

Expansion tank

Cool wat· retu

Smoke →

HOT WATER HEAT

"I think the important thing about the use of heat in homes is that it can be made in one part of the house and taken to other parts," Charles said. "Once every room in a house had to have its own fireplace or stove. Now water or air can be heated in one room and the heat taken to other rooms."

44

"That is called central heating," Jack said. "Our school has central heating. Water is heated in the heater room. It is heated so hot that it turns into steam. The steam rises through pipes all over the school building. It comes into the radiators in every room. The steam heats the iron of the radiators. The warm air from the radiator rises and moves to other parts of the room."

"In some schools, the hot water itself rises into the radiators and heats them," one of the boys said. "It was like that in the school that I went to last year."

"Sometimes hot air is heated in the heater room and blown by a fan into the other rooms," Susan said.

"We have that kind of central heating in our home," said another girl.

Some schoolrooms are heated by stoves that burn wood or coal. How is your schoolroom heated? A trip to a heater room in a school building is always interesting. These are some of the questions that can be answered by such a trip.

1. What fuel is used?
2. What is the source of the fuel?
3. What kind of pipes take the heat from the heater room to the other rooms?
4. What special inventions are used in the heater to make work easier?

You can think of other questions to ask.

"I think the important thing about lighting in homes is that light-colored surfaces reflect more light than dark-colored surfaces," Mary said. "The woodwork and wallpaper in our house used to be dark. No one liked them that way. Now we have painted the woodwork in light colors, and we have light colors in the wallpaper. Mother says it is like having a new home."

"The woodwork and the walls in this schoolroom used to be dark brown and dark green," Miss Hall said.

"It was like that last year where I went to school," said the boy who had told about water rising in the radiators. "Sometimes those who sat far away from the windows had to move over by them to be able to read."

"This room of ours has enough light in all parts now," Charles said. "I suppose that someone used what he knew about science in planning the lighting in this room."

You know that a thermometer is used to measure how hot or how cold a room is. It measures temperature.

A light meter measures the brightness of light in a room. Sometimes a light meter can be found in the school or in the community. It is a good thing to be sure that there is enough light in any schoolroom. Why should there be light in any room? When is there enough light in a room?

This is a light meter being used in a classroom. The one who sits in this place in the classroom does not have enough light. The reading on the light meter shows it. Light is measured in foot candles How many foot candles of light does it show?

Inventions Come Because of Changes

"Compressed air is used in many ways," Miss Hall said. "It is used to make better homes for human beings. Can you think of other inventions that are used to make homes better?"

Everyone could.

"Mirrors are an invention," Mary said.

"Mirrors were invented because people wanted to see themselves," Dave said.

"I use ours every day now when I comb my hair," Jane said. "I think my hair looks better since we placed a mirror in our classroom. Mother says it does. Mirrors bring changes."

"Springs are inventions that make chairs and beds more comfortable," Jack said.

"Chairs are inventions," Tom said. "A rocking chair is a very special invention. I have made a toy one for my sister. It was not easy to make it balance right. I have it at school today. I will show you how I made the rockers."

"A kitchen is full of inventions that make homes better," Dave said. "Everything I know about the science that is used in making machines is used in making things for our kitchen."

"Almost everything I know about the science of heat, water, and electricity is on the chart that Tom, Susan, and I made," Sam said. "Everything we put on our chart can be found out in our kitchen at school or in the one at my home."

"Birds may not change the way they make their homes," Betty said, "but people do. We could keep on talking every day for a month about how inventions have changed homes."

"The modern house near our home has been finished," Jane said. "We have been there to call on the people. I like them very much. I like their house now, too."

Then Jane showed some magazine pictures of furniture like that she had seen in the modern home. "Inventions may seem strange at first," she said, "but after a while we could not get along without them. I would not like to do without electricity, central heating, and running water."

49

"I would not like to be without a telephone," Susan said. "People used to send messages by going to where other people lived and telling them. It took a long time to do that even if they ran to carry the message."

"Indians used to send messages by making smoke signals," Sam said. "Boy scouts send messages now by signals with flags."

"Nothing is as easy as the telephone for sending messages," Susan said.

"I was reading a good book the other day," Dave said. "It tells about Alexander Graham Bell who invented the first telephone. It tells about Edison and Benjamin Franklin and many other scientists and inventors. I wish we could take time to study how people have found better ways of sending messages. We could use many of the books we have, and I know some experiments we could perform."

"We would study about the telegraph, the telephone, the moving picture machine, radio, and television if we did," Tom said.

"I did not mean for us to make a long study about the telephone right now," Susan said. "I was thinking about how homes have been changed by inventions."

"Radios have changed homes very much," Jane said. "You can sit in your room at home and hear news from all over the world. You can hear over the radio what is happening in any other place in the world almost as soon as it happens."

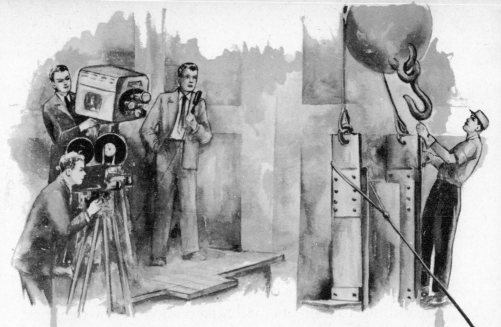

"You can see a thing as it is happening as well as hear it if you have a television set," Charles said. "Of course, someone would have to be near where it is happening to take the pictures and tell you what is happening. Then you could see and hear it on your television set."

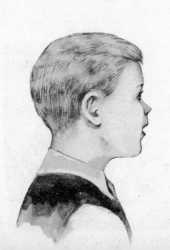

"I should put something about sound in my chart on How Facts of Science Are Used to Make Better Homes," Sam said. "I will do it when we have learned more about it."

"I think we could make a picture chart about sound. We could show how sound has been used by scientists and inventors to make homes better," one of the girls said. "I know something that no one has told about. It is a wonderful invention to make a home a better place in which to live."

This is the picture chart they made. It shows some inventions that no one had talked about. How many of these inventions do you know about?

SOUND

TELEVISION

PHONOGRAPH

PIANO

TELEPHONE

DOORBELL

RADIO

FAMILY ORCHESTRA

Communities of Living Things

A Community

A community of plants and animals is a group of them living together in the same place. A community may be large or it may be small. America with all its people and plants and animals and all the things that are around them is a large community. A pear tree with all its animal visitors and the things that are around them would be a small community.

The plants and animals that live in a community get their food and make their homes in that place. If anything happens to the food of any of them, it may help or harm the others. If anything happens to the homes of any of them, it may help or harm the others. The plants and animals in a community usually depend in some way upon each other.

Some Communities Are Indoors

In the school building where Dave and Betty go, there are twenty or more classrooms like Miss Hall's. Think about this, and try to decide why it is a community. Do Dave and Betty and the other boys and girls in Miss Hall's classroom depend upon anyone but themselves in the school? Do any other people in the school depend upon them? Flowers and other plants are growing in places on the school ground. Do they depend upon anyone or anything? Does anyone or anything depend upon them?

Is your school a community? You know that the answer is yes. In what ways do the boys and girls in your classroom depend upon others in the community? In what ways do others depend on them?

Any home is a small community. The people who live in it depend on one another. They eat and sleep and rest there. If one of them does not put his clothes away carefully, the others see them. If one of them takes a trip, the others hear about it. If the people who live in the home have pets and plants, they take care of them and they enjoy them.

If the home is in a city, it may have other homes all around it. A home in the city may be in a building with other homes. How do city people in one home depend on city people in another home? How do people and pets depend on each other? How do city people depend on farmers? How do farmers depend on city people?

Some Communities Are Outdoors

If the leaves die on the pear tree, the caterpillars that depend on them for food will have to find another home or they will die. If rain washes the good soil away from the roots of the pear tree, the tree will die. If the tree dies, the people who planted it will get no pears from it. Birds cannot make nests in it. Insects cannot use its leaves for food.

A lily pool in a backyard is a small community. Goldfish live in the water. Water lilies grow in the pool. Robins come to the pool to take a bath or to drink. A frog lives near the pool. In what ways do the plants and animals that live near or in the pool depend upon each other? In what ways do they depend on water?

"Our aquarium is a community of plants and animals," Susan said. "We can easily observe it and see how plants and animals depend on each other."

"The plants and animals in our aquarium depend on us, too," Tom said. "We have to help keep the aquarium clean. Sometimes, we must put in fresh water. The animals would not have enough food at first if we did not put some into the aquarium."

An Aquarium Is a Community

"I have learned what a well-planned aquarium is by observing ours," Sam said. "It means that everything in the aquarium seems to depend on the other things. To plan an aquarium well means to keep plants and animals alive and healthy."

"You have to know many things about science to make a well-planned aquarium," Dave said. "We made one at home. My mother said she thought that I had learned many useful facts that helped us keep our plants and animals growing and living together."

"Observing an aquarium is a good way to learn some facts of science," Charles said. "I have been watching the snails for several days. A snail has two eyes that are set up on stalks that can be drawn in or put up. A snail can draw one eye-stalk into its body and leave the other one sticking up."

"I have watched the snails, too," Jane said. "They go up or down the sides of our aquarium and eat the small plants which are called algae. They eat some waste that falls from the fish, too. Our aquarium is a small community where nearly everything depends on some other thing. If there were no water, there would be no fish or snails or algae. If there were no algae and other plants, the fish and snails would have no food that was not put in for them. If there were no snails, the waste and algae would be harmful to the aquarium."

A Well-Planned Aquarium

This is a well-planned aquarium. Look at it carefully. What are the signs of its being well planned?

In this aquarium there are two kinds of fish. One is a goldfish. One is a shiner. In what ways are they alike? In what ways are they different?

In this aquarium there are two kinds of snails. One is a red snail, and one is a black pond snail. In what ways are they alike? In what ways are they different? The red snail has a shell that is a little red in color. The pond snail has a shell that is black. The red snail lays eggs. The babies of the pond snail are born from the adult snails and look like them. You can see the babies of the pond snail in the aquarium. You can see the eggs of the red snail, too. The eggs are fastened to the inside of one of the glass sides of the aquarium. Fish may eat them before they change into young snails.

In this aquarium there are three kinds of plants that you can see. One has feathery leaves. One has a long stem with leaves on all sides of the stem. One is floating on top of the water. How do the leaves of this plant help keep it floating on top of the water?

Boys and girls in any classroom can set up an aquarium. This is the way to set up a well-planned, fresh-water aquarium.

Materials That Are Needed

1. A large tank with glass sides. The tank should be longer than it is wide. It should be about a foot deep. The glass should be cleaned with clear water and a cloth or a sponge. Soap or cleaning liquids and powders may be harmful to the plants and animals that will be placed in the aquarium.

2. Some clean sand for covering an inch or more of the bottom of the tank. The sand will hold the plants in place and give them some food for growing.

3. Some stones to hold the sand and plants in place and to make the aquarium more interesting.

4. A small net for dipping out the animals.

5. A rubber tube or a bent glass siphon for helping to keep the aquarium clean.

6. A pitcher and a pan for pouring fresh water into the aquarium.

7. Four or five pieces of plants that grow in water. They give off something that the animals need, and the animals give off something that the plants need. The animals also eat the plants.

8. Fish. One small fish an inch long needs more than one gallon of water. Too many fish should not be put in an aquarium.

9. Four or five snails to help keep the tank clean.

10. Clean water. If water is taken from a pipe, it should be kept in a pan or bucket for a day or two before it is used. Water for the aquarium should be about the temperature of the room before fish are put into it.

How the Aquarium Is Set Up

1. Be sure that the tank is clean.

2. Pour in the sand and spread it over the bottom.

3. Place the plants in the sand and place stones above the roots. If the plants have no roots, place sand and stones on the ends where roots will grow. This will hold the plants where you have put them.

4. Pour clean water into the tank. Pour the water onto a flat plate held near the sand. Why is that a good way to do it? The water should come to about two inches from the top of the tank.

5. The tank with the water and plants and sand in it should stand for a day before you put the animals into the water.

6. Put the snails and fish into the water. Use the dipping net to lift them into the tank. It is not good for the animals to be handled.

7. Cover the tank with a clean flat piece of glass. Why should the piece of glass be used to cover the tank?

8. Feed the fish at first with food that you can buy especially for them. Uncooked oatmeal is a good food for fish. Do not feed fish every day. Only a small amount of food is needed.

How to Know the Aquarium Is Well Planned

1. If your aquarium is well planned, the plants will begin to grow.

2. If your aquarium is well planned, the fish will not come to the top of the water and open their mouths for air.

3. If your aquarium is well planned, the fish will swim around and eat the food they find in it. They will look well.

4. If your aquarium is well planned, you will not have to do much to keep it clean. If the sides of the glass begin to look green, it is because small plants are growing on them. The plants are called algae. Sometimes water in a pond or on top of a pond looks green. Algae will grow in the water of a well-planned aquarium. Algae are part of the food that the well-planned aquarium supplies for the animals.

5. If you are helping to care for the aquarium, you will not wish to feed the animals in it more than they can eat. No pieces of uneaten food should be left in a well-planned aquarium.

6. If your aquarium is well planned, you will need to put only a small amount of water into it after it is once started. The glass cover will keep the water from evaporating too quickly..

A Terrarium Is a Community

"I should like to have a terrarium in our class-room," Jane said after the boys and girls had been talking about their aquarium one day. "I know how to make one. It will be another kind of community of plants and animals for us to watch."

The others asked Jane to show them how to set up a terrarium. "A terrarium is a place where we observe plants and animals that live on land," Jane told them first. "My father said that terra means land and that aqua means water. Ours is a fresh-water aquarium. The plants and animals in it live in fresh water. We could have a salt-water aquarium. Plants and animals that live in salt water would be put in it. We can make a dry-land terrarium or a wet-land terrarium. I know how to set up a wood-land terrarium. It will be like a little woods."

This is the way that Jane and the others set up a woodland terrarium.

Materials That Are Needed

1. A glass tank like the one that is used for an aquarium.

2. A large handful of charcoal. Charcoal is what is left when wood is not quite burned to ashes. It is easy to make charcoal.

3. Some sand and small stones.

4. Rich, moist, wood soil. You can make wood soil by mixing one part of sand with two parts of leaf mold. Leaf mold is decayed leaves.

5. Small, flat dish to hold water for a pool in the terrarium.

6. Slow-growing plants. Use different kinds of plants. Find out which ones grow well.

7. Animals such as a salamander, small land turtle, toad, land snails, and earthworms. A land turtle is called a terrapin.

8. Water enough to fill the flat dish.

9. A flat piece of clear glass for covering the terrarium.

How the Terrarium Is Set Up

1. Clean the sides and bottom of the tank or jar.

2. Put a large handful of charcoal in the bottom of the tank or jar. Charcoal keeps the soil from turning sour.

3. Cover the charcoal with a layer of sand and small stones.

4. Heat the wood soil in the oven or pour boiling water over it. The heat will kill any harmful insects or plants in the soil. When the soil is cool and dry again, put the soil over the charcoal and the sand and stones. Make one side and one end of the soil in the terrarium higher. This will make some of the soil deeper for larger plants.

5. Set the flat dish in one end of the terrarium. Fill it with water. Make the soil come up to the edge of the dish.

6. Moisten the places where plants are to be placed. Put in the plants and sprinkle them with water after they are planted.

7. Place the flat piece of glass over the tank or jar when you have put the plants in.

8. After the terrarium has stood for a week or two, the plants will begin to grow. Then put in the animals.

9. Flies and ants are good insects to use for animal food. Fruit and berries can be used for food for some of the animals, such as the land turtle.

A Swamp Terrarium

You can make a swamp terrarium. A swamp is a low wet place. Soil for the swamp terrarium should be taken from a swamp. It can be made by mixing one part sand, one part peat moss, and one part small rocks. Peat moss is taken from a swamp. It is plants that have fallen into a thick heap but have not decayed. It is usually sold at seed stores.

A Desert Terrarium

You can make a desert terrarium if you can get the plants and animals that live together in a desert. A desert is a hot dry place. The plants that grow in a desert are different from the plants that grow in a swamp or in the woods. A cactus is a plant that grows in many deserts. Observe that its leaves are different from the leaves of most plants. They are often covered with thorns. If you try to handle a cactus, you may stick a thorn into your hand. If you cut a cactus leaf open, you will see that it has much water in it. What would happen to an animal that tried to eat a cactus? If anything cut open a leaf on a cactus on a hot, dry desert, what would happen to the water in the leaf? Why is a cactus leaf thick and thorny?

This is a desert scene. Observe the different kinds of plants and animals that live together in a desert. A desert is a hot, dry place. There is not much rain in the desert. The plants and animals that live in a desert do not need much water to keep them alive and well.

The places on the earth are not all alike. Sometimes the earth is smooth and sometimes it is rough. You may live where there are mountains. You may live at the seashore. You may live on a desert. You may live where land is smooth. You may live where it is cold most of the time. You may live where it is warm most of the time. Plants and animals live in all these places, too.

What communities of plants and animals live near where you live? The boys and girls in Miss Hall's classroom made many trips to observe the plants and animals that live together in their community. You could do it for your community.

A Secret Place

"I have thought of something for us to do," Charles said to the others in his schoolroom. "We are interested in how plants and animals live together and depend on each other. We could choose a secret place near our school. Then we could observe the plants and animals there at all seasons of the year and in all kinds of weather."

"I know a good place for doing it," Dave said. "It is near enough for us to walk to it at any time. No one seems to go near it. I found it one day when I was collecting seeds."

Miss Hall and the others went with Dave to look at the secret place. They walked across the school yard and down a small hill. They came to a large oak tree beside a small stream. Thick bushes were growing between the secret place and the road. Rocks were between the secret place and the fence behind a house. In one place there was a small, sandy spot beside the stream. Many kinds of plants were growing near by.

"No one will object to our coming here, I am sure," Miss Hall said. "Do you suppose we could learn about this community of plants and animals? Could we learn about the kind of place they need and how they depend on each other?"

"I think it would be better than an aquarium or a terrarium," Betty said. "A terrarium and an aquarium have to be set up inside a room."

"We can learn how life really goes on in nature if we come here at all seasons of the year and in all kinds of weather," Tom said. "I think that Charles and Dave and Betty are right. This is a secret place. It seems to have plants and animals of many kinds. It is a little world of nature already set up for us."

"It looks like a well-planned aquarium or a well-planned terrarium now," Charles said. "The plants are growing. The soil must be good. The water is running along clear and fresh."

"Look," said one of the girls. "Here is a toad sitting under the root of the oak tree."

"Here are some fish in this small pool," one of the boys said, "and a crayfish, too."

This is a picture of the secret place that the boys and girls and Miss Hall decided to study at all seasons of the year and in all kinds of weather.

They made a Notebook for Science about what they observed. They did not tell anyone where their secret place was. They put their Notebook for Science in the Science Fair. Susan and Tom and some of the other boys and girls worked together to make this drawing of the secret place.

Pages from a Notebook for Science

The Notebook for Science that Miss Hall's class put in the Science Fair was interesting to the whole school. If you observe plants and animals living together in communities, you can make pages as interesting as these pages from the Notebook for Science that Dave, Betty, and the others made. The boys and girls made pictures, or cut them from books.

NOTEBOOK OF SCIENCE
By the Boys and Girls
in
Miss Hall's Classroom

COLONIES OF PLANTS AND ANIMALS

Many animals and plants live in colonies. One violet plant may spread its seeds and make a colony of violet plants. The colony will be growing where the plants have the kind of soil they like. Some plants grow in clay. Some plants grow in good garden soil. Some grow in sand. Some grow in shade. Some plants grow in full sunlight.

Bumblebees live in colonies. Honey bees, wasps, ants, aphids, tent caterpillars, and hornets live in colonies. Oysters live in colonies, too.

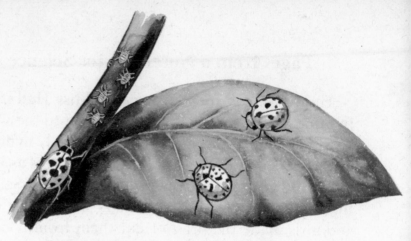

LADYBIRD BEETLES AND APHIDS

Ladybird beetles are useful insects. They eat aphids. Aphids are tiny insects that suck the juice from the stems or leaves of some plants. Aphids live in colonies. Sometimes you can see them on a cherry, an apple, or an orange tree. Many of them live together on some wild evening primroses we know. They look like scales on the end of the stem. They stick their bill or sucking tube into a plant and live on its sap. They kill the plant after a while. Anything that will help destroy aphids is useful. The ladybird beetles are useful as soon as they come from the eggs. When they first come from the eggs, they are caterpillars. Caterpillars are also called larvae. The larvae or caterpillars change into another form of the insect. The ladybird beetle and the larva from which it comes both eat aphids.

There are many kinds of aphids and of ladybird beetles. We could not find out how many aphids a ladybird beetle or its larva will eat, but we have seen them eating aphids from the stems of the evening primroses.

ANTS AND APHIDS

Evening primroses get their food from the air and the soil in the place where we go to see communities of plants and animals. Aphids suck their food from the stems of the evening primroses. Ladybird beetles and the larvae from which they come eat the aphids. People who like evening primroses and cherry, apple, and orange trees do not like aphids. They do like ladybirds.

Ants use aphids. A sweet, sticky liquid comes from the bodies of aphids. Ants eat the sweet, sticky liquid that is given off by the aphids. We have seen ants feeling the aphids with their antennae. Antennae are feelers on an ant's head. They are like the antennae on a butterfly's head. When the aphid feels the ant's antennae moving over it, it gives out more of the sweet, sticky liquid. We laughed and said that the ant was milking the aphid. Sometimes the ants keep aphids as carefully as a farmer keeps his cows for milk. Ants have sometimes carried eggs of the aphids into the ground and kept them safe during the winter. In spring they bring the eggs out and put them on a plant stem or leaf which will supply food for young aphids. If an ant tries to milk an aphid that has supplied its sweet, sticky liquid to another ant, it hurries away to find an aphid that has not had its liquid taken away.

71

MORE ABOUT ANTS

Ants live in communities or colonies. Some kinds of ants make slaves of other kinds of ants. They find the home of the ants they use for slaves and go into it. If they do not get into a fight or if they win the fight, they take larvae to their own home and care for them. When the larvae turn into ants, they become slaves and do the work of the home after that. They are not taken out to fight other ants. Once we were turning over stones in the place we know when we found a nest of the brown ants that make slaves of the black ants.

Ants sometimes fight if other ants want the ground they are living in. A fight between two colonies of ants may last for several days. At night the ants go to their homes. Next morning the fight begins all over again. It goes on until one colony wins.

A COLONY OF BUMBLEBEES

We have watched a colony of bumblebees in the place we have chosen to watch all the year around. One day in spring we saw the mother bumblebee, or queen, trying to find a place for her nest. At last she found a place in the ground where a field mouse had once had its nest. We watched her carry food from the flowers to store in her nest. We found in a book that she lays eggs on the mixture of food in the nest. We know that other bumblebees hatched from the eggs she laid, for we saw them flying about gathering food for other young bumblebees. We were careful not to catch the bumblebees, for they have a sharp sting. Bumblebees are useful insects, for they carry pollen from one flower to another. Pollen is the dusty looking part of a flower that helps make good seeds on flowers of the same kind.

The Secret Place at Different Seasons

Autumn, winter, spring, and summer are the seasons of the year. How do communities of plants and animals change with the changing seasons?

1. In Autumn

The days are getting shorter in autumn. The sun shines for a shorter time each day from about the middle of September until about the middle of December. The nights are longer than the days. The plants need sunlight for making food. As the days grow shorter, what happens to the leaves of weeds and bushes and trees? Are there seeds on some of the plants? Cold nights with frost begin to come in autumn in many places. Frost kills the leaves on some plants. Even a little frost will kill the leaves of tender plants like a tomato. It takes a heavy frost and freezing weather to kill the leaves of some plants. Some plants do not bloom until autumn. The leaves of some plants stay green all winter. They are called evergreen plants.

In autumn animals get ready for winter. Squirrels gather acorns from the ground under the oak trees. They hide them in holes in trees or in the ground. Moths make cocoons. Some insects go into the ground to make cases in which the caterpillar changes its form. Some birds gather together into flocks before flying away to a warmer place. Toads and frogs and salamanders and snakes go into holes or under stones and logs in autumn.

2. In Winter

The shortest days of the year come in winter. Many plants do not get enough sunlight for making food. The bulbs and roots of some plants rest safely underground during the cold and icy days and nights of winter. Coverings of fallen grass and leaves and snow help keep them safe. Many plants have made seeds that have been scattered on the ground. Some of these seeds are not killed by frost.

In winter many plants do not get enough sunlight to make food. Leaves have fallen from the trees and plants that are not evergreens. The leaves lie upon the ground where they will decay and turn into leaf mold. Leaf mold helps make some kinds of soil. The branches of the trees and bushes are bare, but look closely at them. You can see buds from which new leaves and blossoms will grow. The buds are covered over with a protection of gray or brown scales on the tree or bush.

Fewer animals can be seen in winter. Insects are safe in cocoons, in the ground, or under bark and leaves and stones. Some of the insects have laid their eggs and placed them where the cold of winter will not harm them. Earthworms have gone deep down into the ground where it is not frozen. Squirrels, bears, and chipmunks come out of their winter homes only on sunny warm days. Snakes, toads, crayfish, frogs, lizards, and other cold-blooded animals have gone into holes in the ground or under rocks or logs.

Some of the birds have gone away to warmer places for the winter. Other birds may have come for a short time. Some birds stay all year long in the same place if they can find food enough there. Rabbits and mice do not go away in winter. They always seem to find food and a warm place to live even in the coldest weather.

Communities of plants and animals have their own special ways of living through the winter with its ice and snowstorms and frozen ground.

This is a picture of the secret place that Dave and the others have chosen for observation. It is a picture of the place in the middle of winter. What signs of life do you see in the picture? Where are the fish that lived in the pool in the tiny stream? What has the rabbit found to eat? How would a rabbit be harmful in an orchard of young apple trees in winter?

76

3. In Spring

The days are becoming longer in spring. The sun shines for a longer time each day. The nights are shorter than the days from about the middle of March until about the middle of June. Spring comes earlier in some places than in others. When do the plants begin to show above the ground as they grow from the bulbs underground where you live? Sometimes in some places the green of plants can be seen pushing up through snow. Plants need sunlight for making food. As the days grow longer, what happens to the buds on bushes and trees? Sometimes if days are warm for a long time in early spring, the buds of leaves and flowers begin growing too soon. A frost may come. If a frost comes after the buds of the flowers on trees have grown too much, no fruit will form on the trees. Farmers and other growers of crops watch the weather carefully in the spring. They read the weather reports in the newspapers and listen to the weather reports that come over the radio. Fires that make much smoke are sometimes built in orchards when there is danger of a heavy frost. Sometimes plants are covered to protect them from the frost.

Spring is the time for plants to start growing from bulbs, roots, seeds, and buds. New leaves and blossoms come out. Much of the world turns green again in spring.

Many new animals are born in spring. Lambs, calves, colts, young pigs, and chickens can be seen

77

on many farms. Birds build nests, lay eggs, and hatch their young in spring. Some birds that have been in warmer places come back in spring. Insects come from cocoons and eggs or from their winter homes. Snakes and other cold-blooded animals come out and sit or lie in the warm sunlight. Colonies of ants, wasps, bees, and other insects begin to move about everywhere. Baby animals can be seen also.

This is a picture of the secret place that Dave and the others have chosen for observation. It is a picture of the place in early spring. What are the signs of early spring that you see in the picture? Are there young birds in the robin's nest? Are there some plants that you would not see in the picture of the same place in autumn? What is the squirrel eating?

4. In Summer

The longest days of the year come in summer. Plants have all the sunlight they need for making food. Some plants are in bloom. Some plants have already made their seeds. Fruit is ripe on many of the berry bushes. Trees have all their leaves.

Every plant and every animal is busy in summer. It is the best time for growing. Plants have long days of sunlight for making food. Roots bring water from the ground up through the stem of the plant to its leaves. The leaves take carbon dioxide from the air through tiny openings in them. Carbon dioxide is a gas that is in the air. Leaves that are green change carbon dioxide gas and water into sugar. The plants change the sugar into starch. Starch is one kind of food that plants make. They also make protein, but scientists do not know exactly how they do it. Protein is a food that animals need for growing. Human beings need the proteins that plants make. Plants store the foods they make in seeds, roots, stems, and other parts. The change from carbon dioxide and water to sugar can take place only in sunlight. Starch and protein are made only when plants are growing. That is why summer is the time for plants to make food. Plants supply the food that keeps animals alive. In summer animals can find all the food they need if the weather and soil and air keep plants growing. Bears and some other animals eat so much in summer that they are fat enough to live all winter without food.

If no rain falls in summer, the plants cannot make food. If the plants cannot make food to store in seeds, roots, stems, and other parts, all animals get thin. Some of them die.

Some animals eat only special kinds of plants. In any community of plants and animals, an observer can watch the animals choosing the special food they need. Rabbits do not eat onions or tomato plants. They eat cabbage and lettuce and clover. Some plants will grow only in special soil. Plants and animals depend upon each other and upon the soil, the air, and the water in their community. You can find out about this by watching an aquarium, a terrarium, a garden, a window box, or a place outdoors that you choose.

This is a picture of the secret place that Jack and the others chose for observation. What are the signs to show that it is summer? What are the signs to show that the plant and animal life is growing well together in this community?

Communities of Plants and Animals Change

"The plants and animals in our secret place change with the seasons," Miss Hall said after observations of the life there had been going on for almost a year. "Does anything else cause changes in the life there?"

"Weather does," Jane said. "If we do not have rain for a month or two, the pool and the little stream do not have water in them. The fish and the crayfish move away or die. Insects that live near water go away or die. Weeds and grass begin to grow where the water was."

"If it rains for a long time, the water in the little stream rises and covers the ground near by," Sam said. "Then the plants that are covered by water die. The nests of the field mice and the bumblebees are flooded, and the mice and bees have to find new homes. Moles do not make their burrows in wet ground."

"Sometimes there are no berries or seeds and the birds go away," Betty said. "I think that the supply of food makes more changes in plant and animal communities than anything else."

"The amount of sunlight makes a change in the communities of plants and animals," Susan said. "Some plants live best in the shade."

"The plants and animals themselves make changes in their communities," Dave said. "Some plants and some animals are pests. People make changes in communities of plants and animals, too."

Pests

"When is a plant or an animal a pest?" Sam asked.

"I have made a collection of harmful insects," Dave said. "I collected mosquitoes, flies, grasshoppers, cabbage butterflies, potato beetles, and a cotton boll weevil. They are all pests."

"Ants are pests sometimes," Betty said. "When they come into the house and get in the food, they are pests. If they make their homes in a flower garden, they are pests."

"Moles are pests in a flower garden or in a grassy lawn," Susan said. "Mice and rats are pests, too."

"Weeds are pests in a garden or in a field of corn, wheat, or cotton," one of the boys said.

"Birds are pests sometimes," Tom said. "They are pests if they eat vegetables in a garden. Robins eat cherries, and then they are pests. Father says robins are pests when they eat earthworms. Earthworms are useful. They make holes which let air into the soil. They help mix the soil."

"Most birds eat so many harmful insects that they seem more useful than harmful," Sam said. "I would never call a bird a pest."

"You would if you were a farmer and it came into a field and ate some of the crop you wanted for yourself," one of the boys said.

"The bird needs food, too," Sam said.

"Every living thing needs food," Tom said. We all know that. I suppose an animal or a plant is a pest if it eats the food that some other living thing needs."

"A ladybird beetle is a pest for aphids," Betty said. "I suppose ants would have more food if there were no ladybird beetles, but we would not. Aphids are harmful to fruit trees and to many other plants that are useful to human beings."

"A plant or an animal is also a pest to human beings when it is poisonous to them or when it harms them," Jane said. "Poison ivy does not use the food I want, but it makes my hands and face swell if I touch it. Mosquitoes do not use the food I want, but they bite me and they may carry disease."

"Now I begin to understand about pests," Sam said. "A plant or an animal is a pest to another plant or animal when it is harmful to it or when it takes the food that the other animal or plant needs for itself."

"In a well-planned aquarium there is enough food for the plants and animals to live and be comfortable," Betty said. "The plants need the animals, and the animals need the plants."

"That is the way it is in a well-planned terrarium, too," Susan said.

"It is the way it is in the secret place we chose," Tom said. "When nothing happens to the supply of food, the plants and animals seem to get along well together."

"Plants and animals use one another for food," Jack said. "That means that some of them are harmful to others. Some of them harm humans, too."

"Human beings can talk and think," Dave said. "When they find out that a plant or an animal is harmful to them, they find ways to destroy it. They clean up garbage. They spray to kill flies. They drain swamps and spray to destroy mosquitoes. They put out traps and poisons to destroy rats and mice. They pull out poison ivy by the roots or spray it to destroy it. Sometimes they shoot harmful animals."

"I wish we could make some charts to show what we have learned about the plants and animals that are most harmful to human beings," Dave said. "We could find pictures of them and tell how they are harmful."

"We could make a few charts of some of the animals that are most useful to us, too," Tom said.

"Farm animals are useful to human beings and so are all kinds of crops in farms and gardens, but everyone knows how useful they are," Susan said.

"Most trees and flowers are useful to human beings in some way, but we have talked about many of them," Charles said. "We would not need to put them in our charts."

"If trees make too much shade, they kill the smaller bushes and trees that grow near them," Susan said.

"Everything is useful or harmful to some other thing, I think," Jane said. "We will need to think about that when we make our charts."

"I wanted the charts to be about plants and animals that are most harmful to humans," Dave said.

"I wanted to make a few charts of plants and animals that are most useful to human beings," Tom said. "If we think about human beings and the kind of communities they like, we will know what to put on the charts."

"We can look in our science books for some of the information we need, and we can ask Miss Hall," Betty said. "I think Dave and Tom have made good suggestions."

The others decided to do what Dave and Tom had suggested. They used the books of science in their Science Corner. They used other books from their school library. They used their observations of the aquarium, the terrarium, and the outdoors. They performed a few experiments, and they asked many questions at home and at school. Their charts were interesting.

Useful Plants and Animals

Pine Tree — Cow — Meadowlark — Fish — Bee — Black Snake

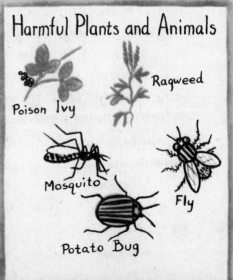

Harmful Plants and Animals

Poison Ivy — Ragweed — Mosquito — Fly — Potato Bug

Clippings on a Bulletin Board

Newspapers often tell about what is being done to destroy some pest. They also tell about some especially useful plant or animal. The boys and girls in Miss Hall's classroom have a bulletin board. They put clippings from the newspaper on the bulletin board. Sometimes they find pictures and stories in magazines. They clip them and place them on the bulletin board along with the newspaper clippings.

While they were learning about some plants and some animals that are especially useful or harmful to human beings, the bulletin board was so interesting that children from other classrooms in the school came to see it.

On the next pages are stories and pictures about other useful and harmful animals.

Honey Bees

Honey bees are useful to human beings because they make a sweet food that most people like. It is honey. The bees make the honey for food for the young bees and for themselves during the winter season when no flowers are in bloom. They make so much honey that people can take part of it without harming the bees.

Honey bees are useful in another way. They carry pollen from one flower to another. Pollen is the kind of golden dust that you see in most blossoms. Seeds of plants start in the blossoms. To make seeds from which new plants will grow, pollen from one blossom must be carried in some way to another blossom on the same kind of plant. Wind may carry the pollen from one blossom to another. Honey bees and other insects that go to the flowers for food carry the pollen, too. Some fruit trees will not make fruit if the pollen is not spread by wind or insects. The plants and the bees depend on each other. Human beings depend on them both. A honey bee is harmful only if it stings.

Honey bees work together to do all kinds of things that are good for their community. A community of honey bees is usually very large. It may contain as many as ten thousand different bees. It is something like a city. There is one important difference between a community of human beings living in a city and a community of bees living in a hive. A human being may change the kind of work he does in his community. A bee never changes from the kind of work it does.

A community of bees is called a colony. In the colony are different kinds of bees, and each kind does its special kind of work. Every colony of honey bees has three kinds of bees.

First of all, the colony of bees has workers. They are the ones that make honeycomb. They gather the food from the flowers and store it so that all in the community have enough to eat. The workers keep the home of the colony clean, and take care of the eggs and the baby bees. They protect the colony from enemies. The workers are smaller than the two other kinds of bees. Most of the bees in any colony are workers.

Some bees in the colony are a little larger than the workers. They do no real work and are called drones. One of them mates with the queen before she lays her eggs. The queen is a much larger bee than the workers or the drones. She is the mother of the colony. She lays the eggs from which the baby bees come.

If it were not for the queen and the drones there would be no baby bees to keep the colony alive and growing. The workers live only about a month after they begin working and so there must always be a new supply of them. Drones do not live long either. The queen bee is busy during all the warm weather laying eggs. On some days she may lay as many as six thousand eggs. When the queen is ill or injured so that she cannot lay eggs, she is stung to death and thrown out of the colony by the workers. A new queen is hatched from some of the eggs. Sometimes several queens are hatched in a colony. The old queen fights the new queens, for no colony has more than one queen at the same time.

If the home is crowded, the old queen sometimes takes some of the workers with her to a new home. She leaves a new queen in the old home. A swarm of bees is made up of the workers and the old queen leaving the old home.

The workers in a colony of honey bees are busy from morning to night during all warm and sunny days. They keep the community going by doing their special work.

SWARM

BEEHIVE

HONEYCOMB

WORKER

QUEEN

DRONE

Birds Useful to the Farmer

Birds found in one part of the United States are sometimes similar to birds that are found in another part. The common phoebe is found in the eastern part of the United States and the black phoebe, that is very much like it, is found in the western part. The yellow-billed cuckoo is found in the eastern part of the United States and a bird very much like it, the California cuckoo, is found in the western part. The western violet-green swallow is similar to the barn swallow in the eastern part of the country.

All of these birds eat insects. The meadowlark eats bugs, beetles, grasshoppers, and a few flies and wasps. It also eats the cotton boll weevil and other harmful weevils. It eats cutworms. Cutworms are white grubs that are the larvae of May beetles and chinch bugs. All those insects are pests to the crops of farmers. In a book about common birds it is easy to find out what insects are eaten by the other birds on this list of useful birds. You will find out that some of them eat mosquitoes. One of them, the yellow-billed cuckoo, even eats hairy caterpillars. In every Science Corner on the shelf for books there should be a book about birds.

Some of these birds eat the seeds of harmful weeds. The meadowlark and the bobwhite do. The bobwhite eats seeds of crab grass, smartweed, chickweed, beggar lice, and ragweed, among many others. The bobwhite is a very useful bird, and any farm on which bobwhites make their homes will have fewer harmful insects and weeds. From books about birds, you can easily find out what seeds other birds eat.

Some of these birds eat a few berries and seeds of crops, but all of them are so useful that they should be protected. Birds very much like these ten birds are found in many parts of the United States.

HOUSE WREN

CHICKADEE

PHOEBE

MEADOWLARK

RED-WINGED BLACKBIRD

DOWNY WOODPECKER

YELLOW-BILLED CUCKOO

NIGHTHAWK

OBWHITE

BARN SWALLOW

A Toad

A toad may live near almost any house that has a yard. It finds a cool place under a root or a rock for a home. The toad does not live in a colony. It lays eggs on water and gives no care to the baby toads. Its home is not really a home, but only a place where it sits and sleeps. The toad has a long, sticky tongue. It catches its food on its sticky tongue. It can flick its tongue out so fast that you can hardly see it.

The toad eats insects. It eats flies, mosquitoes, ants, beetles, termites, and many other harmful insects. The toad is not harmful in any way. A toad in a garden is almost as useful as a hoe.

Toads are called frogs by some people, but everyone who has looked closely at them can tell a toad from a frog. The toad has a skin which is usually dry and rough. Frogs have a smooth, moist skin.

Cabbage Butterfly

The cabbage butterfly that we usually see was brought from Europe about a hundred years ago. It has spread all over the United States now. The cabbage butterfly can be seen in almost any garden and in every garden where cabbages are growing. Its four wings are white and have one or two black dots on them. The front and hind wings are nearly the same size. The cabbage butterfly does not eat the cabbage or other plants like it. It lays eggs from which caterpillars hatch. The eggs are laid sometimes one in a place and sometimes several in a row. The caterpillars that come from the eggs may grow to be about an inch long. They are greenish in color. These caterpillars are pests. They eat the leaves of cabbages. The caterpillars do not live in colonies although several may be found eating the same leaf.

Termites

Termites are insects. They look a little like ants and sometimes are called white ants, but they are not ants. They live in colonies the way ants and bees and wasps do. The termites have a king and a queen. The queen lays the eggs from which new termites come. The queens of some kinds of termites lay 30,000 eggs daily. In every termite colony there are also workers and soldiers. The workers take care of the eggs and make the home large enough for all the members of the colony. The soldiers do the fighting. They protect the workers who are out searching for food.

Termites eat wood. They burrow into wood as easily as moles burrow into soil. Wood is their food. In warm climates termites are harmful to houses. They eat the wood of the house and may harm it before the owner of the house knows they are near. They live in dark places and get into the wood by going up through tunnels that they build of mud to reach the wood. Termites are not useful in any way.

94

Moles

Moles live underground. They have pin-point-sized eyes. They have very strong paws. They dig long holes or burrows underground usually near the surface of the soil. They are mammals and their babies are born alive from the mothers.

The mole is a harmful animal. It eats earthworms which are useful in the soil. Moles dig burrows under the surface of grassy lawns, and often the grass dies. Mice run through the burrows of the moles and eat bulbs of some plants. The mice eat the bulbs of tulips.

Moles eat some white grubs and other insects that live in the soil. The fur of moles is sometimes used for making warm coats. In those ways moles are useful animals.

Moles live in colonies underground. It is not easy to get rid of moles when they begin to make burrows in a lawn.

95

Grasses That Are Pests

The three grasses on the next page are pests to farms and gardens. They are different from the grass in a good lawn.

Johnson grass has a tall straight stem. Its leaves are tough. The roots go deep into the ground. If one small piece of root is left in the ground, another plant will usually grow from it. If Johnson grass starts to grow in a field, it is hard to get rid of it. The grass is spread from roots and by seeds.

Quack grass is sometimes called witch grass. It has tough leaves and low, tough stems. The roots of quack grass make a thick mat just under the surface of the soil. They grow down into the soil for as much as three or four inches. They are hard to get rid of if they get a good start in the soil. Even a small root left in the ground will start a whole new colony of quack grass. The grass is spread from roots and by seeds.

Crab grass is low, spreading, and tough. Its roots make a tough mat under the surface of the soil. Crab grass is spread by roots and by seeds. To get rid of crab grass, one must dig out all the roots or use a special weed killer.

The grasses such as Johnson, quack, and crab are pests because they crowd out other wanted plants. Their roots are so matted that other roots cannot find a place among them. These grasses take the place of useful grasses on a farm.

The chief use for grasses like these is that they will keep soil from washing away when heavy rains come. Other grasses that farm animals will eat also keep soil from washing away. Animals will eat Johnson grass, and it is used for hay in some states.

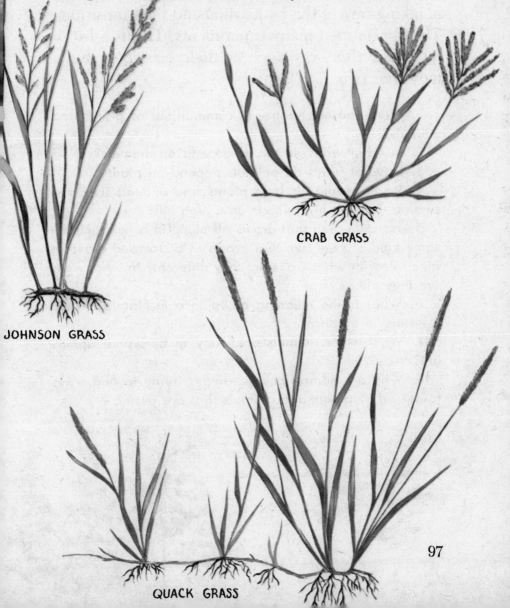

JOHNSON GRASS

CRAB GRASS

QUACK GRASS

Balance and Change in Communities

Miss Hall and the boys and girls in her classroom had many experiences on their trips to the secret place for observation. They had many experiences in taking care of their aquarium and their terrarium. They performed many experiments. This is a list of questions that was kept in their classroom for a month or two.

1. What causes changes in communities of plants and animals?

2. In what ways do plants depend on animals?

3. In what ways do animals depend on plants?

4. Do the same kinds of plants and animals live in a swamp that live in a woods on a high hill?

5. Is a pine tree that grows all alone in a field like the same kind of pine tree that grows in a crowded grove of pine trees? In what ways are they different? In what ways are they alike?

6. What is the meaning of Balance in Nature? When is nature in balance?

7. What other animals are likely to be where aphids are? Why?

8. Why are human beings always trying to find ways to get rid of plants and animals that are pests?

Plants and Animals Use Each Other

"Balance in nature means that plants and animals which live together find enough of everything they need to keep themselves and others like them living there," Miss Hall said. "Balance means that there are enough plants and enough animals for them all to use one another."

"Sometimes if there are too many animals, all the plants are eaten. In Australia there are too many rabbits now. The rabbits are destroying the crops, and the farmers want to get rid of them," Dave said. "Once there were no rabbits in Australia. Then someone brought a few into the country because he thought they could be used for food. Today rabbits are pests there, because nature is not balanced."

"Some farmers leave a few stalks of wheat or other grain in a field for the birds," Betty said. "The birds will eat insects that may destroy crops. They will eat seeds of weeds. Some of the birds may eat mice and other pests. As long as there is enough food for the plants and for the animals, the balance of nature is kept."

"If plants and animals use each other, why don't they all get used up?" Charles asked.

"They keep on producing others like themselves," Jane said. "If they are not all killed, others will come from them."

"Plants and animals have ways for protection against most of their enemies," Sam said.

How Some Plants Are Protected

Susan was arranging a bouquet of flowers for the classroom while the others were talking. Some of the flowers were roses on long stems.

"Ouch!" Susan said, as she picked up one of the roses. "These thorns are sharp! Why do the stems of roses have thorns on them?"

Sam suggested that roses need protection in some way. Then he suggested that they try to find how plants of many kinds are protected.

"Some plants have thorns on them," Tom said. "Susan knows that roses do. Blackberry vines have thorns on them. Cactus plants have thorns on them, too."

"Some cactus plants do not have thorns," Betty said. "We have one in a pot at home that does not."

"I think most of them do," Tom said. "All the cactus plants that grow wild on the desert or in fields have thorns. If they did not, they could be nibbled by animals and all the water in them would evaporate."

"Some plants have sticky liquids in them," Dave said. "Milkweed plants do. Some plants have a disagreeable odor. The skunk cabbage does."

"Some plants have leaves that are tough," Betty said. "Animals won't eat them."

"Why do plants need to be protected from being put into bouquets or from being eaten by animals?" Susan asked.

"We know some facts of science that will help us answer that question," Betty said. "Flowers grow on many plants so that seeds can be made. If seeds are not made, no more new plants like the ones that made the flower will grow. Flowers are important to the life of plants."

"Betty is right," Tom said, "and I know another fact of science that will help us answer Susan's last question. Green leaves are the factories in which plants make their food. If green leaves are all eaten from a plant and new ones cannot be grown quickly, the plant will not be able to make its food. Leaves are important to the life of plants."

Susan and the others began to understand why plants that have protection of some sort can continue to live.

Leaves and plants are protected in many ways. These are some of the plants that have ways for protection. What ways do they have? Make a chart of the ways you find.

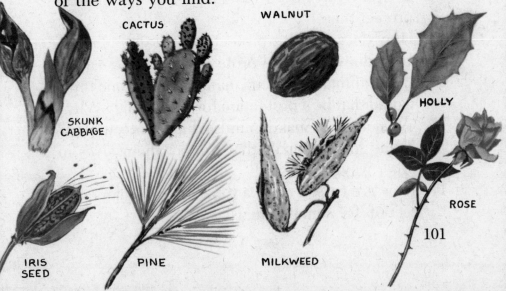

CACTUS

WALNUT

HOLLY

SKUNK CABBAGE

IRIS SEED

PINE

MILKWEED

ROSE

101

How Some Animals Protect Themselves

Animals protect their lives in many ways. Among living things there is a struggle to keep on living. Animals produce others like themselves so that they may continue to live and grow. These are some questions to make you think about animals and their ways of protecting themselves.

1. In what ways do claws help protect cats?
2. How do horns help protect goats?
3. How does a tail help protect a cow?
4. In what other ways is a cow protected?
5. How do teeth help protect a dog?
6. In what ways is a horse protected?
7. How do wings help protect birds?
8. How does the color of some animals protect them?
9. In what ways can a frog protect itself?
10. Why is it hard to see a toad in a garden?
11. In what ways does the shape of some animals protect them?
12. How does a rabbit protect itself?
13. How does a squirrel protect itself?
14. If any animal produced many babies at one time, would that be a protection for the animal? Why?
15. What animals make sounds which protect them?
16. Name some animals that protect themselves in other ways.
17. How are ears, a nose, a tongue, and feelers protection for some animals?

These are animals of many kinds. Some of them are named in the questions on the page before this. In what ways does each of these animals protect itself?

Communities of Unseen Plants and Animals

"The sides of our aquarium became covered with this green material too quickly," Charles said. "I know this green material is something that grows in still water where there are not enough animals to eat it. I would like to know more about it."

"The green material is algae," Miss Hall said. "Algae are simple plants. They grow anywhere in still water that is of the right temperature and that is open to the sun. They make the green covering that forms on the inside of the glass of an aquarium. Algae make their own food from air and water if sunlight is present.

"Molds are also tiny plants. You cannot see single plants well without a microscope. Sometimes you can see colonies of them on bread and fruits. Sometimes you can see mold on a fish in your aquarium. Molds do not have flowers and they do not make seeds. They produce others like themselves by means of spores. The spores will make mold on any material that is formed from living things if the material is in the right kind of place. Molds do not make their own food. This is mold on a piece of bread."

"I have seen mold on bread and other food at home," Susan said. "When does it grow best?"

That was a good question. It can be answered by performing this experiment.

An Experiment

1. What You Want to Know
   When does mold grow best?

2. What You Need
   Five slices of bread

3. What to Do
   Toast one slice of bread and keep it dry.

   Put another slice of bread on a plate and keep it moist. Keep the two slices of bread at the same temperature for a few days. Place another moist slice of bread on a plate and keep it in the refrigerator. Place a moist slice of bread on a plate and keep it in a warm place. Place a slice of moist bread on a plate and keep it hot and moist if you can. Observe the slices of bread for a few days. Does more mold grow on one of them than on the others?

4. What You Find Out
   Do moisture and warmth seem to make mold grow best?

Bacteria are also tiny plants. They can be seen with a microscope. They grow almost everywhere. They are in soil, in the water of ponds and streams, and even in milk. Bacteria are on all foods and in the air. They grow in all places if the temperature and moisture suit them. This is what you might see if you looked at the bacteria in a drop of water under a microscope.

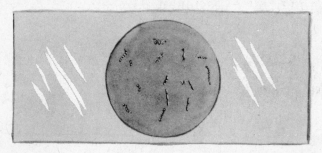

Dave and the others know that pond water contains tiny animals. If you look at a drop of pond water under a microscope you will probably see small animals swimming about. You may see one of them about to reproduce itself by dividing into two animals of the same kind. This is what you might see if you looked at the tiny animals in a drop of pond water under a microscope. The water in a well-planned aquarium is very much like water in a pond.

Louis Pasteur

Louis Pasteur became a famous scientist. He was born in France, and his work as a scientist has been useful to the whole world.

Louis Pasteur was born before scientists or anyone else knew much about molds, algae, or bacteria. If anyone saw a patch of mold on a piece of bread or decaying fruit, he did not know that it was something alive. No one had thought of its being a plant or an animal. Not many people had heard of bacteria.

In the place in France where Louis Pasteur went to work after he was through college, beet roots and grapes were grown for making wine. Bacteria grows in all kinds of fruit juices. We know that now, but in Pasteur's day people thought that juices just turned sour. Pasteur was curious to know about the making of wine, which was a great French industry.

What caused the juice to turn sour? What caused milk to turn sour? Those are the questions that Pasteur asked himself. He decided to do experiments to find the answers to his questions. He set to work in an old laboratory in Paris. He had a microscope and almost nothing else with which to work.

Pasteur had ideas, and he made apparatus to suit his needs. He found out that bacteria are in the air. He found out that if fresh juice could be kept away from air, it would not turn sour. He found out that wine would stay sweet and fresh if it was heated and put in airtight bottles.

If milk is heated to about 140 degrees for 30 minutes and then cooled very quickly and put in airtight bottles, we say it has been pasteurized. Where did we get the name pasteurized? What is pasteurized milk? Will it stay fresh for a long time if it is kept in bottles in a refrigerator?

Pasteur did many other experiments to show that diseases are caused by germs that are in the air. Disease germs are harmful tiny living plants or animals. Pasteur found that germs reproduce themselves as all living things do.

Silkworms in France were attacked by a disease. Pasteur found out that a germ produced the disease. Dogs had rabies, or went mad. A germ causes rabies. Diphtheria and typhoid fever are spread by living germs. All those diseases can be prevented if you stay away from germs. That is not easy to do, but it is easy to kill the germs of those diseases. Pasteur found out how to do it.

You can perform some experiments that will tell you some of the things that Pasteur found out.

Experiments with Bacteria

Experiment One

1. What You Want to Find Out
   Can bacteria and mold be planted in milk?
2. What You Need
   Bread on which bacteria and mold have formed, test tubes with corks, milk, needle or pin, heat.

3. What to Do

The mold on the bread should have spots of yellow, red, or purple on it. These are spots where bacteria are growing along with the mold.

Take three test tubes and boil them and their corks in water for five minutes. Fill them nearly full of milk that has been boiled. Boiling kills the bacteria and mold in milk.

Take the needle or pin and hold its point in heat for a minute. Be careful not to burn your fingers. A cork makes a good handle for the needle or pin when you hold it in the heat. Why?

Let the point of the needle or pin cool. Do not let it touch anything when it is cooling. Now touch the point to one of the yellow, red, or purple spots on the moldy bread. Put the point that has touched the spot on the bread into the milk in one test tube. Take the point away from the milk and place a cork in the test tube. Do the same thing for one of the other test tubes. Cork the third test tube, but do not put any bacteria and mold in it. Set the test tubes away where you can observe what happens.

4. What You Find Out

Does the milk in all the test tubes change color? In which ones does it change color? How do you know that no bacteria and mold were in the milk or the test tube or on the cork after they had been boiled? Did you plant bacteria and mold in the milk? How was it done?

Experiment Two

1. What You Want to Find Out
Can bacteria be planted by touching food with a finger that is not clean?

2. What You Need
Gelatin and a place to prepare it
Two plates
A finger and a place to wash hands

3. What to Do
Prepare the gelatin as if you were going to eat it, but do not put sugar in it. Pour some of the gelatin into each of the two plates and let it cool.

After the gelatin is cool let someone touch the surface of the gelatin in one of the plates with his unwashed finger. Then ask him to wash his hands well and then touch the surface of the gelatin in the other plate with a clean finger. Make a record of the place where he placed his finger on each plate.

Cover the plates of gelatin to keep dust away from them. Let them stay for three or four days in a warm, dark place. At the end of that time take them out and observe what has happened.

4. What You Find Out
What has happened to the gelatin where the unwashed finger touched it? What has happened to the gelatin where the clean finger touched it? Why should hands be washed before food is handled?

Experiment Three

1. What You Want to Find Out
   Are there bacteria in the air?

2. What You Need
   Potato
   Plates
   Glass jar for covering potato

3. What to Do
   Cut three slices of potato and place one on each of three plates. Let each slice remain for an hour where air will be blown over it. Cover each slice with a glass jar. Make a record of the date. Set the plates with the covered slices in a cool and rather dark place. Observe the slices every day and make a record of any changes you find. Why does the covering over the slice of potato keep it from drying out?

4. What You Find Out
   Did you observe any change in the surface of the slices of potato? What is the color of the spots you may have observed? What is their shape? Is a colony of bacteria growing on the potato?
   Set the slices of potato with the spots on them in sunshine. What happens to the bacteria?
   Are there bacteria in the air? Why should food be kept covered? What happens to bacteria when they are placed in sunshine?

Useful and Harmful Bacteria

Bacteria that kill silkworms are harmful. Bacteria that cause milk to spoil and dogs to have rabies are harmful. Some kinds of bacteria and some microscopic animals cause human beings to become sick. They are disease germs.

Some bacteria cause dead plants and animals to decay. They are useful when they do that.

Bacteria that live on the roots of clover and other similar plants are useful. Nitrogen is a part of the air. Plants need it to grow. Plants cannot take nitrogen from the air. Bacteria that live on the roots of clover and other similar plants can take nitrogen from the air in soil.

Little knots on the roots of clover and other plants are made by the bacteria. You can see the little knots on the roots of white, red, and other clover plants in the picture. Beans, peas, and some other plants have them, too. All other kinds of clover plants have the same kind of little knots on their roots. Look at them closely to find out more about them.

112

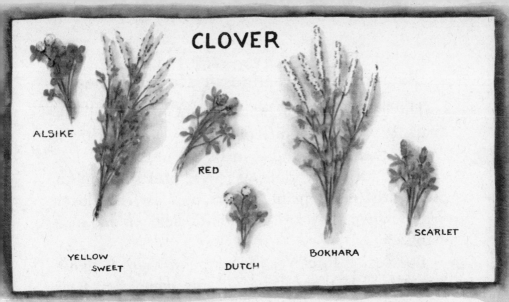

CLOVER

ALSIKE

RED

YELLOW
SWEET

DUTCH

BOKHARA

SCARLET

"We can see the little knots on the roots of clover plants," Harry said to the others in Miss Hall's classroom. He was observing the roots on some clover plants that he had brought back from a trip. "We cannot see the bacteria in them. The bacteria belong to the community where clover plants grow just as much as bees do. Bacteria are just as useful to the clover plants as bees are."

"Harry is right," Miss Hall said. "Bacteria are useful to the clover plants. They take nitrogen from the air and return it to the soil. Before the nitrogen is returned to the soil, the clover plants use it for making their growth. When the clover is eaten by animals or cut by men to be stored away for food for their animals in winter, the roots may die. Then the nitrogen goes back into the soil."

"I think I will collect all the kinds of clover I can find in our community," Kate said. "It is one of the most useful plants I have heard about."

113

Balance and Change in Communities

This is a balanced community of plants and animals. It is a community of clover plants and bees. What other plants and animals are in it?

There are many kinds of clover plants and all of them are useful plants. Farm animals eat clover plants when they are green in a field or dry in a barn.

Bees come to clover blossoms for there is much sweet food in them. Who eats the honey that bees make? They depend in some ways on this balanced community.

Clover plants are spread by seeds. They live in a community because they spread their seeds near by.

The bacteria on clover roots that take nitrogen from the air and put it in little knots on the roots of the clover plants belong to this community.

Sunshine, air, water, and soil are necessary for this community of plants and animals.

Look around you for other balanced communities of plants and animals. What are necessary to keep them balanced?

Living Things Need Food

An Experiment in Feeding Rats

Dave brought four young white rats to the classroom. The young rats were four weeks old. They had been born in the same litter. A litter of rats is all the babies that are born at one time from a mother rat. A litter of kittens is all the kittens that are born at one time from a mother cat. What is a litter of pigs or a litter of puppies?

"The mother white rat had four babies in the litter," Dave said. "I brought all of them for our experiment."

The four young rats were as alike as four animals ever are. Their fur was smooth. Their eyes were bright. They moved about easily. They were healthy young animals, for their mother had given plenty of milk for all the babies in her litter.

"I gave the mother rat good food," Dave said. "I gave her milk, eggs, carrots, whole wheat seeds, and a dried mixture of whole wheat bread, liver oil, and tomato juice. I put her cage where plenty of warm sunshine would reach it. I gave her fresh water and made a cosy warm bed in her cage."

Jane and Sam and some of the other boys and girls worked hard to make cages for the young rats. Each cage was made of wire. Young rats that are healthy have sharp, strong teeth and can gnaw through wood easily. Each cage had a cosy, warm place where the young rat could sleep. Each cage was large enough for the young rats to run about and get plenty of exercise. On each cage there was a strong handle so that the cage could be moved into sunlight without upsetting anything in it. In each cage there was a pan into which fresh water could be poured.

Two young rats were placed in each of the cages. Here they are in the cages that Jane and Sam and the others made. Because the cages and the young rats in them looked so much alike, the children made signs and put the signs on the cages.

The two rats in Cage One were to be fed only white bread with no crust. They were to live in one of the two cages that were exactly alike. They were to be given fresh water and placed in fresh sunlight just as the rats in Cage Two were. The rats in both cages had plenty of room for running around and getting exercise.

The two rats in Cage Two were to be given plenty of the same kind of food that Dave had given their mother. Their food was to be milk, eggs, carrots, whole wheat seeds, and a dried mixture of whole wheat bread, liver oil, and tomato juice.

In the experiment, only the kind of food was to be different. The experiment was to show whether the kind of food made a difference in the ways the rats grew. The boys and girls kept records every week of the weight of the rats.

"Will the rats in Cage One be hungry?" Jane asked.

"They will have all the food they can eat," Sam said. "They may not grow well on the food they have, but they will not be hungry."

The experiment was to last for six or eight weeks.

Miss Hall said it would take that long to see what difference the kind of food made.

"While we wait to find out what happens to the rats, why don't we find out more about food for plants and animals and ourselves?" Mary said.

Miss Hall and the boys and girls in the room thought Mary had a good idea; so they set to work.

117

Living Things Need the Right Kind of Food

Dave and Betty and the others in Miss Hall's classroom know that plants will not grow in some kinds of soil. They have planted seeds in washed, clean sand, in clay, and in good garden soil.

Sand is made of small bits of rocks and shells. When it is washed clean, all the bits of decayed plant and animal life are taken away from it. Clay is soil that has almost no decayed plant and animal life in it. It is usually packed hard under a surface of good soil. It may be deep down in the ground. Sometimes it may be on the surface if heavy rains have washed the good topsoil away. Good garden soil can be made by mixing decayed plant and animal life with sand and clay.

Dave and Betty and the others had planted seeds in pots with different kinds of soil in them and had watched the plants grow from the seeds. You can do it, too. Keep the plants watered and in sunshine. In which pot do the plants seem to grow best? Sometimes plants get all the food they need from water or from air. A water plant in the aquarium in Miss Hall's classroom will grow. Where does it get its food?

"If you have poor soil, you have to add something to it to supply food for the plants," said one of the boys who had lived on a farm. "Farmers and people who work in gardens know this."

Fertilizers are food for plants.

"Fertilizers for plants, that grow on farms and in gardens, cost a large amount of money every year."

"I have watched men in the spring putting fertilizer on the lawns and around the trees and shrubs in the park," Susan said. "Mother says they are feeding the plants."

This is a field of corn. The land is poor land and that means that the soil has little food for plants in it. The farmer did not put fertilizer on the field. What tells you that the plants are not healthy?

This is another field of corn. Only a fence separates it from the field in the other picture on this page. What tells you that the plants are healthy? The soil in this field is good. It has enough food for plants in it. The soil may have been good soil, or the farmer may have made it good by adding fertilizer to it.

119

Dave and Betty and the others in Miss Hall's classroom know that animals need food if they are to stay well and to keep on growing. They have cared for many different kinds of pets in their classroom. Most of them have cared for pets at home, too.

They have put out food for birds on a feeding tray near their schoolroom window. They have watched animals in the secret place they have chosen for observation. They have seen those animals catch and eat the food that each needs. They have watched birds feed their young in the nest.

"The foods that animals eat are different just as the animals are different," Sam said one day when they were all talking about how every living thing needs food. "It is the same for plants, too. Some insects take the juices from other animals and from plants for their food. Some animals give milk for their babies. They are mammals. Some birds eat insects and other animals, and some eat seeds. Some birds eat both seeds and insects or other animals. Some animals eat meat and some eat plants. Some plants need one kind of soil and some need another kind. I have observed all kinds of communities of plants and animals. I am beginning to know about the foods that the different plants and animals need. Different kinds of foods that we eat, or that plants and animals eat, have different substances in them. I am beginning to know a little about substances and the chemicals that are in them."

120

"What are substances and chemicals?" Jane asked.

"I will make a small booklet for you," Miss Hall said. "I will try to tell in my booklet enough about substances and chemicals so that you can begin to understand the words when you hear them used and to use the words yourselves."

This is the small booklet that Miss Hall made. It caused the boys and girls to ask many questions about the foods they eat. You might like to make Miss Hall's booklet into a booklet for yourself. You could draw pictures for different parts of it.

SUBSTANCES AND CHEMICALS

Most of the substances we use as foods are solids and liquids. Bread, meat, potatoes, rice, beans, cheese, butter, and apples are all solids. A solid substance has a definite shape. We know a loaf of bread by its shape. We know a potato by its shape. We know an apple by its shape.

Some of our foods are liquids. Milk, cooking oil, and vinegar are liquids. A liquid pours. A liquid takes the shape of the container into which it is poured. A liquid does not have a definite shape.

Every substance known to us is either a solid, a liquid, or a gas. Water, although it is not a food, is used in preparing food and preserving food. It may be a solid, a liquid, or a gas. Water is also found as one of the substances in many of the foods that feel dry to our touch.

121

A whole apple feels dry, but it has much water in it. Many fruits and vegetables contain water in a liquid form. Much of milk is water. Water is an important substance for all life.

Some substances may be easily changed from one form into another. Water is a substance in liquid form. If water is frozen in any way, it becomes a solid. Ice is water changed into a solid form. If water is boiled, some of it changes into another form. It becomes a gas in form and is called steam. When the water is removed from milk, a liquid, the milk becomes a solid, called powdered milk. Butter, a solid, may be melted to form a liquid.

Milk is a liquid that may be frozen to form a solid. Then we call it ice cream.

A kitchen is a good place to observe the three forms to which water and other substances can be changed.

When a change in the form of a substance takes place, the substance must be heated or cooled.

Any substance is made up of one kind of chemical or of several chemicals. Water is made up of two chemicals. They are hydrogen and oxygen. Sugar is made of three chemicals—carbon, hydrogen, and oxygen. Starch is made of the same three chemicals that make sugar.

Butter is made of three chemicals—carbon, hydrogen, and oxygen. The amount of carbon, hydrogen, and oxygen is not the same in fat, sugar, and starch.

Meat is made of several chemicals—carbon, hydrogen, oxygen, nitrogen, sulfur, and phosphorus. Milk is made of calcium, carbon, hydrogen, oxygen, nitrogen, sulfur, and phosphorus. The minerals and vitamins in foods are also chemicals.

You can show that a piece of bread has chemicals in it. Put some pieces of bread in a test tube. Heat the test tube over a flame. Hold the test tube in the position shown in the picture when you are heating it. Drops of water come from the bread. Water is made of two chemicals—hydrogen and oxygen. The black material left in the test tube is carbon.

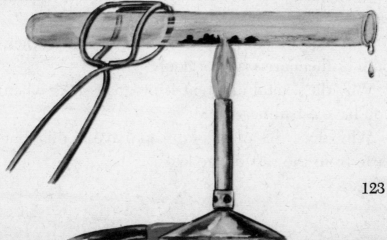

We eat substances, we breathe substances, and we drink substances. We eat, breathe, and drink chemicals. We ourselves and all other living things are made of chemicals. Also things that are not alive are made of chemicals. Everything in the world is made of chemicals.

When we prepare food in our kitchens, changes in substances are taking place. Some of the changes are changes in form. We dissolve sugar in milk. This is a change. We cut carrots into cubes. This is a change. We squeeze juice from an orange or some other fruit. This is a change.

There are other changes that take place in a kitchen. We cook carrots. We scramble eggs. We toast bread. We fry bacon. We bake a cake. In these changes something happens to the substances in the food that makes it different from the substance with which we started. Most of the cooking changes that take place in food make it more useful for the body. Cooking often gives food a better taste, too.

The boys and girls read Miss Hall's booklet. They did the experiment and observed changes in foods at home. They talked about substances and chemicals. They asked many questions.

Why does bread taste different from cake when both of them are made of flour?

Why do several different fruits taste alike when you have a bad head cold?

Why does the crust of bread have a different taste from the rest of the loaf?

124

Changes in Substances

Charles brought a piece of wax to school. Wax is a soft substance, but it is in a solid form in this picture. How can Charles make the piece of wax change its form?

Living things grow and change. Things that are not alive do not grow. They do not make changes in themselves. Changes can be made in the forms of substances. Charles used power to make changes in the piece of wax. He changed its shape by pressing upon it with his hands. The muscles in fingers, hands, and arms have power. They can be used to make changes in substances. Many machines are used to make changes in the shape of substances. Lead can be beaten into another shape by using a hammer. You can think of other ways to change the shape of materials or substances.

What makes changes in the forms of water in a kitchen? How can Charles change the piece of wax into liquid form? What is needed to melt ice?

What makes air move? Air is not alive. It cannot move itself. It is a substance. Does difference in heat cause air to move from one place to another? What is wind? What makes changes in the direction of the wind?

This glass rod is hard. What could be done to a glass rod if anyone wanted to change its shape? What is being used to make glass soft in this picture?

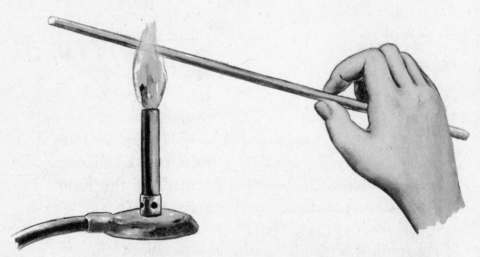

"Changes in substances are made by using power or by using heat," Sam said. "Plants and animals make changes in substances. Plants make their food by taking chemicals from the air and soil. They need water and sunlight for growing. Do water and sunlight help plants change substances?"

Experiments to Find Out about Some Chemicals

The boys and girls in Miss Hall's classroom talked about substances. They talked about chemicals, too.

"Sunlight, air, and water are needed by most growing plants and animals," Jane said. "I know that, because I have watched plants and animals growing. I would like to find out how a plant makes food for itself."

"I want to know what some of the chemicals in foods are," Sam said. "I have some chemicals for performing experiments. I want to use them for answering some of our questions. We also have some chemicals in our Science Corner. We could use them, too."

Jane and Sam started the others upon these experiments that answer some of their questions.

1. How Can You Find Out if Starch Is in a Substance?

Iodine is a chemical. You need some iodine and several different kinds of substances. These are the substances you need—a lump of starch, a cube of sugar, a slice of cooked potato, a green leaf, a cooked carrot, and any other cooked vegetable.

Place a drop of iodine on the lump of starch, and find out what color the starch turns. If starch is in any substance, iodine will turn it the color that it turned the lump of starch. Try placing a drop of iodine on the substances you have. Is starch in any of them?

2. Is Sunlight Necessary to a Plant for Making Starch?

You need a large green leaf on a growing plant and two pieces of black paper. The pieces should be about two inches square. Use a paper clip to fasten a piece of black paper on both sides of the large green leaf on the growing plant. The black paper keeps out sunlight. Keep the leaf with the black paper on part of it in full sunlight for four or five hours.

Remove the covered leaf from the plant. Soak the leaf in alcohol to take out the green color. Take the leaf out of the alcohol and pour iodine on the leaf.

Is sunlight necessary to a plant for making starch?

Plants Take Chemicals from Air and Soil

"I know that some foods have starch in them," Charles said. "I understand a little about how chemicals are taken from the air and used by green plants in making food for the other new plants that will grow from them. I know that a farmer sometimes puts fertilizer on his soil. Fertilizer usually has many chemicals in it. How do the chemicals get from the soil into the plant?"

You can easily find out how it happens. You need a glass jar, red ink, and a stalk of celery with leaves on it. Pour red ink into the jar. Place the cut end of the celery stalk in the ink. Observe for a day to see what happens to the celery stalk and leaves.

Where do you first see the ink in the celery? Make a record of how it travels up into the stalk and leaves of the plant.

Choose a plant with roots, stem, and leaves. Pull it from the pot or garden. Wash the roots clean and place the roots of the plant in inky water. Make a record to show how the colored water travels in the roots and the plant.

Chemicals in the soil are mixed with water and travel to the leaves of plants just as the ink does.

129

Water Changes Some Other Substances

"Chemicals from fertilizers will not do any good for the plants if they are not mixed with water," said the boy who had lived on a farm.

"I suppose that is because only liquids can be taken from the soil by roots of plants," Jack said. "You cannot see chemicals in water, but we know they are there. Miss Hall's booklet told us that water is made of two chemicals. Hydrogen and oxygen are both chemicals. They are in pure water. Water usually has other chemicals in it."

"I know that water dissolves sugar and that I cannot see the sugar when it is dissolved," Mary said.

You can show easily that water dissolves sugar.

An Experiment

Fill a drinking glass with water. Place a cube of sugar in the water. Cover the glass with a handkerchief. Let the glass stand for ten minutes. Take the handkerchief away. The cube of sugar is gone.

The cube of sugar could be seen when it was placed in the glass of water. The small particles of sugar were packed together to form the cube.

If sugar is placed in water, the sugar mixes with the water. When they are mixed, we say that the water has dissolved the sugar.

Solids from Liquids

Dissolve some sugar or salt in a glass of water. Pour the water into a shallow bowl. Observe it for several days.

The water evaporates, leaving behind the sugar or salt. Most solid substances do not turn to a gas at room temperatures. Most liquids evaporate or change to a gas at room temperatures.

Minerals in Water

Place some drinking water in a shallow dish. Let the water evaporate. A small ring of solid material will be left in the bowl. This ring of material is a mineral. In some communities the drinking water contains many minerals dissolved in water. Sometimes the minerals in water make rings of solid substances in wash bowls or cooking pots.

Our Bodies Take Chemicals from Food, Air, and Water

The human body has many parts. Each part of the body has a special job to do. Food is taken into the body through the mouth. Teeth are in the mouth for chewing food. The tongue helps mix the food with juices that come into the mouth when food is being eaten. Food is made of chemicals. So are the juices in the mouth. Muscles help pull the chewed, moist food through a long tube into the stomach. The stomach is a strong muscle. It mixes the food with other juices. Chemicals in those juices help digest the food. To digest food means to change it so that it can be used by the body. Only parts of food that can be dissolved in some liquid can be digested and used by the body. Not all parts of all food can be digested. The waste part of food, or the part that cannot be digested, passes on out of the body. The part of the food that is used is taken into the blood and carried to all parts of the body.

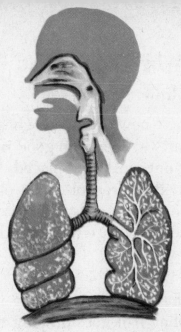

Air is taken into the body through the nose. In the nose the air is cleared of dust, warmed, and moistened. Then the air passes down the windpipe into the lungs. Blood circulates all through the walls of the lungs. Oxygen is taken from the air into the blood in the lungs.

After some oxygen that the body needs has been taken from the air, a strong muscle helps push the air out of the lungs. It pushes the air from the lungs through the windpipe and through the nose out of the body. Then air pushes back to fill the lungs again. This is called breathing.

Sometimes air is breathed into and out of the body through the mouth. The mouth has no ways to warm, moisten, and clean the air such as the nose has. If something is wrong with your nose, you may have to breathe through your mouth.

133

Why Do We Eat?

1. We Eat to Grow

A car must have new tires, new wheels, and many kinds of new parts to keep it in good running order. Parts that wear out must be replaced. It is the same with us. Our bodies are not made of rubber and metal substances but of cells. Cells wear out. They must be replaced if we are to live and grow.

2. We Eat to Get Energy

A car must have gasoline to keep it running. It uses more gasoline if it goes on long trips or keeps running for a long time. When the gasoline tank becomes empty, more gasoline must be put in. It is the same with us. We cannot use gasoline in our bodies for energy, but we can eat foods that give us energy to do work.

3. We Eat for Health

A car must be kept in good condition. A car is a machine whose parts work together smoothly if the machine is well cared for. It is the same with us. If we are healthy, all the parts of our bodies work together. Our teeth are clean and not decayed. Our skin and hair are clean and shining. Our eyes are bright. We look healthy.

"We eat because we grow and change, because we have work to do, and because we feel better when we are healthy," Sam said.

134

"When I go to the cafeteria where I have to choose the food I will eat, I sometimes do not know what to choose," Tom said.

"Our cafeteria has a good chart to help us choose the right kinds of food," Susan said. "We could bring it to our classroom and study it."

Jack went to the cafeteria. In a short time he came back with this chart.

WHAT FOODS HAVE YOU PLANNED FOR TODAY?

1. Green and yellow vegetables
   One or more servings every day.

2. Oranges, tomatoes, raw cabbage, grapefruit, and salad greens
   One serving every day.

3. Potatoes and other vegetables and fruits
   Two servings every day.

4. Milk and milk products
   At least three glasses of milk every day in some form.

5. Meat, poultry, fish or eggs
   At least one serving every day, three or four eggs a week.

6. Bread and cereals
   Three or more servings every day.

7. Butter
   At least two tablespoonfuls daily.

EAT SOME OF EACH OF THESE SEVEN KINDS OF FOOD EVERY DAY.

What to Eat for Growth

The boys and girls looked at the chart that had come from the cafeteria.

"What we choose for lunch depends on what we have eaten for breakfast and what we plan to eat later," Jane said. "We must have different kinds of food for different needs."

"We need to grow, to have energy, and to keep healthy," Dave said. "We eat to keep growing. I have found out that proteins help us grow. Meat, milk, fish, eggs, and some vegetables are rich in proteins."

This is a drawing that some of the boys and girls in Miss Hall's classroom made to show foods that are rich in proteins. Is milk one of the foods that help you grow?

FOODS THAT ARE RICH IN PROTEINS

Every day you should eat some food that is rich in proteins. Proteins are substances that contain certain chemicals. These foods are rich in proteins.

What to Eat for Energy

Heat is one kind of energy. If we eat for energy, we must eat food that will produce heat in the body. Sugar and starch will produce heat in the body. They produce heat for they combine with other chemicals in the body and burn.

Fat is another substance that will produce heat in the body. Fat is oil, and nearly everyone knows that oil will burn.

Many foods have some form of sugar in them. These are some that do. They are good to eat for energy. Is milk one of them?

Many vegetables and cereals have starch in them. These are some that do. How can you tell when starch is in a fruit, seed, stem, root, or leaf of a plant? Look on page 127 to find out if you do not know.

Many plants have oil in their seeds. Crush a pea-
nut or a wheat seed on a clean piece of paper. What
do you find on the paper after the pieces of seed
have been brushed off? These are plants that make
oil and store it in some of their parts. You can find
out other plants that make oil and store it in their
parts.

Many animals store fat in their bodies. The fat
comes from the plants the animals eat. These are
some oils or fats that come from animals. From
what animals do these fats come?

BACON

CREAM

BUTTER

SUET

LARD

138

What to Eat for Health

You may grow and you may have energy, but you may not be well. You must eat something more than proteins, sugars, starches, and fats. You need something in your diet that will keep you healthy. Your diet is the food you eat. Minerals, vitamins, roughage, liquids, and other substances should be in the diet for health.

The minerals we eat are found in plants and animals. The plants take the chemicals from air and soil after the minerals have been mixed with water. The animals get minerals from plants. These plant and animal products are rich in minerals. Is milk one of them? Iron and calcium are minerals.

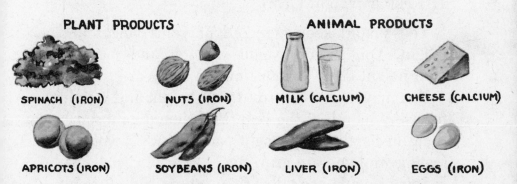

PLANT PRODUCTS   ANIMAL PRODUCTS

SPINACH (IRON)   NUTS (IRON)   MILK (CALCIUM)   CHEESE (CALCIUM)

APRICOTS (IRON)   SOYBEANS (IRON)   LIVER (IRON)   EGGS (IRON)

Green and yellow vegetables and all yellow fruits such as oranges, lemons, grapefruit, and cantaloupes should be eaten to help keep you healthy. They are all rich in minerals and vitamins.

Some of all of the seven basic foods should be eaten every day for growth, energy, and health.

What Do You Eat?

"We know what we are feeding the two rats in Cage One," Susan said. "We know what we are feeding the two rats in Cage Two. We can see that the rats in the two cages are not growing in the same way. I think we should begin to study the foods we are eating."

"We know what we should eat every day," Harry said. "The chart from the cafeteria showed the seven kinds of foods that we should eat every day. We could keep records of what we eat and of how we grow."

You can do the same thing. This is a way to do it.

1. Keep a Weight Chart

You should keep a record of your weight and height. You should weigh yourself and measure your height three or four times in the year.

You may keep a record of your height and weight for every month of the year. You should gain something in height and weight each month if you are feeling well and are growing.

Some people are taller than others. Some weigh more than others. If you feel well and if you grow some each month, you are probably healthy. Do not worry if you are not as tall as someone else. Do not worry if you do not weigh the same as someone else. You should be careful to eat the right kinds of foods to gain in height and weight from month to month.

140

Miss Hall was able to tell each boy and girl in her classroom about the right weight for them.

A weight record was a part of the record on the four rats that the boys and girls in Miss Hall's classroom kept. They could tell by the records whether the rats were getting the right kinds of foods.

2. Keep a Record of Your Diet

You should keep a record of your diet for three weeks. Then you can be sure that you are eating what you need for growth and health.

Compare what you eat with the chart of the right kinds of foods. Do you eat some of the right kinds of foods every day? Do you eat too much food between meals? Do you have plenty of milk every day?

A diet record was a part of the record that the boys and girls in Miss Hall's classroom kept on the four rats in the feeding experiment. They could tell by the diet record what kinds of foods the rats were getting.

3. Keep a Health Record

Other things than food are needed to keep you well and growing. You need rest. You need exercise. You need to keep clean.

Copy this chart and keep a record on yourself. It is a health record. It also has a record of the food you eat. Mark an X under the day if you did what you should have done.

My Health Record
For One Week

Name _____

Month _____

Date _____

	S	M	T	W	T	F	S

Food

I ate   breakfast

        noon meal

        evening meal

I ate some of these foods

    Green and yellow vegetables   1.

    Oranges, tomatoes, salad greens 2.

    Potatoes, other vegetables, fruits 3.

    Milk and milk products   4.

    Meat, poultry, fish, eggs   5.

    Bread and cereals   6.

    Butter   7.

Rest

    I had 10-11½ hours of rest

Exercise

    I played or worked

Cleanliness

    I brushed my teeth

    I washed my hands before each meal

    I combed my hair

    I bathed

    I cleaned my fingernails

    I wore clean clothes

Why Should We Drink Water?

"We have been keeping our weekly health records. I am beginning to know what the right kinds of foods are, but why should we drink several glasses of water each day?" Charles asked. "Water is not a food."

"Plants and animals need water to help keep them alive," Mary said. "We know that for we have performed many experiments and have had many experiences to prove it."

"I like a drink of fresh water when I become hot from playing hard," Sam said. "If no water is taken into my body, none will come out on the skin to evaporate and to make me cooler."

"I suppose water is needed in the body to help chemicals mix with each other," said Jack.

"Water helps wash food waste from my body," Sam said.

"Water is useful to human bodies in all the ways you have named," Miss Hall said. "It is sometimes harmful to us, too."

"Impure water is harmful," Jane said. "On a picnic we always boil water before we drink it unless there is a sign saying the water has been tested and is safe. Boiling kills the germs in water."

"Disease germs cannot be seen without a microscope. They may be in clear water. I can show you how to make water clean and how to kill the disease germs in it, too," Sam said.

What Sam Showed the Class about Water

1. Making Water Clean

Many cities take their drinking water from large rivers. The water of many rivers is quite muddy. You may prepare some muddy water by putting a few lumps of clay in a jar of water and shaking it hard. Let the muddy water stand for a while. Some of the clay will go to the bottom. Not all of the clay in the water will go to the bottom, even if the water stands for a long time.

Prepare some muddy water in a jar and this time put in about one tablespoonful of lime and the same amount of powdered alum. Stir the mixture. Observe that a white jelly-like material forms and goes to the bottom of the jar. As it goes down, all the clay is drawn down with the jelly-like material.

Cities whose supply of water is muddy use chemicals to clean the water. Then this clean water is run through a bed of sand. We say it is filtered. This removes all undissolved materials that are in water.

2. Sand Filter

It is easy to show how a sand filter cleans water. Use a lamp chimney. Tie a piece of thin cloth over the top end of the chimney. Then turn the chimney over. Put about two inches of coarse gravel into the chimney on top of the cloth. Add two inches of fine gravel, then two inches of coarse sand, and about two inches of fine sand. The sand should be clean. That means it should be washed with water before it is used. Pour some muddy water through the sand filter. Catch the filtered water in a glass. Is it clean? Filtering water through thick beds of sand also removes some bacteria. It does not make it safe for drinking.

3. Adding Chlorine to Water

Drinking water which contains live germs is dangerous. Drinking water which contains dead germs is harmless. Bacteria or disease germs which may be present in the water may be killed by boiling the water. This costs too much for large amounts of water so instead of boiling it, a gas known as chlorine is added to the water. Chlorine is a chemical. Chlorine gas is poisonous, and large amounts should not be breathed. It takes only a small amount of chlorine to make the water safe.

"Sam has shown us how to make water clean and how to kill the bacteria and germs in it," Charles said. "That shows how to get water that is safe for drinking. Why should we drink several glasses of water each day?"

"Your body is made up of cells," Miss Hall said. "All cells need water to do their work. You should also drink water each day to help wash the waste material from your body."

"If I drink three glasses of milk every day, must I drink several glasses of water, too?" Charles asked.

"Milk is also a liquid and it will take the place of water in supplying the body with liquid for helping the cells grow," Miss Hall said. "Other foods like soup supply water for the body, too."

One good reason for eating fruits and vegetables is that they have so much water in them. You can find out that vegetables and fruits contain much water by squeezing juice from them. Orange juice is mostly water. How much does the juice in one orange weigh? Are all oranges the same size? How much water can you get from a cucumber? You cannot squeeze all the water from any fruit or vegetable.

"Leaves and stems of plants have water in them," Susan said. "Roots and stalks of plants do, too."

"The sap from a maple tree and the juice from a cane plant are mostly water," Jack said. "They carry the chemicals to different parts of the plants just as blood in a human body does."

146

Plants and Animals Make Chemical Changes

Plants make their food from chemicals that they get from the air and from the soil. Animals do not make their own food but they eat plants or other animals that have eaten plants. Human beings are a kind of animal and do not make their own food. They use plants and other animals as food. All food really comes from plants.

The animal eats the starch that is stored in the plant when it eats leaves, stems, roots, or seeds. The plant had stored the starch for its own use or the use of new plants that would grow from it. The animal used the starch to help it grow. It changed the starch back into sugar by chewing it.

Chew a piece of bread made from the starch which is in the seeds of corn, wheat, and other grains. The saliva in your mouth changes the starch in the bread back into sugar. You can taste the sweetness after you have chewed the bread for a short time.

Suppose you are eating breakfast one morning. This is the food you have. It is a good choice of food for breakfast. For each of these foods, find out about the plant that made it.

PINEAPPLE JUICE

MILK

BACON

SCRAMBLED EGG

BUTTERED WHOLE-WHEAT TOAST

BLACKBERRY JELLY

147

This is a pineapple plant. The pineapple juice you have for breakfast comes from fruit like the fruit you see on this plant.

This is a cow. The milk you usually drink comes from cows. The cows eat grass and other plants or grain. Grain is the seeds of plants. The cows make milk. They make the milk to feed their own babies. Some cows make enough so that human beings can take some of it from them and use it for themselves. The milk is made from the chemicals in the plants. When the cow eats the plants, she chews and digests them and makes changes in the chemicals to produce milk. Cream and butter are fat from milk that came from cows.

148

This is a pig. Bacon is made from the flesh of a pig like this one. The pig eats corn or peanuts or acorns or other seeds or roots or plants. The corn and other plants have fat in them. The pig eats them and the chemicals are changed into its own flesh. Bacon comes from the plants that the pig and other animals eat. This is a plate of breakfast bacon. It does not look either like a pig or like a plant, but it came from them.

These are hens. You can see the eggs that the hens have laid in the nests. The eggs that you ate for your breakfast came from hens. The hens ate seeds and other parts of plants, and the chemicals in the plants were changed into chemicals that made the eggs. Hens often eat insects and other small animals. What do the insects and the other small animals eat? If farmers want hens to lay many eggs, they give them special kinds of food.

149

This is a field of wheat. You can see the seeds on the stalks of wheat. The wheat seeds are gathered. They are ground into flour. The flour is mixed with other substances and is made into bread. The toast you had for breakfast came from plants. The butter on the toast you ate for breakfast came from milk, and you know where milk is made.

These are blackberry plants. The fruits are shiny and juicy and black. Their juice is taken out, boiled with sugar, and made into jelly. The sugar came from plants, too. This is a glass of blackberry jelly.

150

Choosing a Balanced Diet

"I have been watching our rats in the two cages every day and food does make a difference," said Susan. "Sometimes I used to think that my mother was making me eat food just to please her."

"It is not easy to choose just the right kind of food for every meal," one of the boys said, "but I think I know now what a balanced diet means. It means some of all the foods that help us grow, give us energy, and keep us healthy."

"We need meat and milk to keep us growing," Jack said.

"Older people need them to replace the cells that wear out in their bodies," Miss Hall said.

"We need vegetables to help keep us growing and to give us energy," Jane said.

"Now I know what parts of vegetables we eat and why we eat them," Charles said. "We eat the seeds of some vegetables because they contain starch, and starch is a food that gives us energy. Seeds contain oil, and oil gives us energy, too."

"We eat the roots of some vegetables such as beets, carrots, and turnips partly for vitamins and the rough parts," Jack said. "I know why we should eat some of them raw. Cooking may take away some of the value of some foods."

"We eat the stems of some vegetables such as celery, asparagus, and rhubarb," Mary said. "We eat them for their rough parts and for minerals. We eat them for vitamins and for starch."

151

"We eat the leaves of vegetables such as cabbage, lettuce, and spinach," Tom said. "The greener the leaves the better they are for our health."

"We eat the fruit of many plants," Sam said. "Seeds are the fruit of plants, but we eat the fruit of many plants for the part of the plant around the seeds. Cherries, oranges, melons, peaches, berries of all kinds, pears, grapes, apples, and all kinds of fruits can be named. We eat them because we like the taste of the fruit and because the fruit juice gives us energy, vitamins, minerals, and other things we need."

SEVEN BASIC FOODS

Some of all of the seven basic foods should be eaten every day for growth, energy, and health.

After they had studied foods and had made records of their diets for several days, the boys and girls in Miss Hall's class made a picture chart of the seven foods that should be eaten every day.

"I think I know now how to choose a more balanced diet when I go to the cafeteria," Tom said.

"If human beings choose something from the different parts of the plants that are grown for food and if they add meat, milk, and liquid to the diet, they will always choose a balanced diet," Miss Hall said.

"I wish the rats in both cages had been given balanced diets for the six weeks of our experiment," Jane said.

The End of an Experiment in Feeding Rats

These three pictures show what happened to the two rats in Cage One. Look at the second part of each picture to see how the young rats appear in Cage Two. The rats in Cage Two have been given a balanced diet. It is the kind of diet rats try to find for themselves when they are not in a cage.

UNBALANCED DIET

BALANCED DIET

TWO WEEKS

TWO WEEKS

FOUR WEEKS

FOUR WEEKS

SIX WEEKS

SIX WEEKS

"I do not like to look at the rats in Cage One," Jane said. "We have all learned many things by performing the experiment in feeding. Now the experiment is ended. I want to do something to help the rats in Cage One."

"If we feed them a balanced diet for a few weeks, will they be healthy again?" Susan asked.

"We can try it to find out," Jack said.

They did try it, and this is what they found out. What makes you think that the two rats in Cage One are more healthy than they were? What differences can you see between them and the rats in Cage Two?

A Lunch in Miss Hall's Room at School

Miss Hall and all the boys and girls decided to prepare lunch in their classroom. They worked together to plan what they would have to eat.

This is the menu.

> Hot vegetable soup, crackers
> Tuna fish sandwich, whole wheat bread
> Egg sandwich, whole wheat bread, chopped parsley
> Raw carrots, celery, tomatoes, and cucumbers
> Grape juice
> Cottage cheese and jelly sandwich

The schoolroom had two outlets for electricity. Tom said he would bring an electric hot plate. There was an electric hot plate in the Science Corner of their room, so they had two places for heating soup.

Jane and Sam and some of the others said they could bring the cans of soup. Water could be heated on the hot plates. Pitchers of water could be used for the water supply. Pans and jars would be all right for a place to wash the dishes and to pour the waste. A table was set up to be a part of the kitchen. This is the kitchen in the schoolroom.

Committees were chosen to prepare the different parts of the menu. The day before the lunch, Susan and Sam and some of the others made apple jelly for the cottage cheese and jelly sandwiches. In the morning they put the apples in a pot with some water and boiled them just long enough so that the juice would run out. They hung the cooked apples in a cloth bag over a pan to catch the juice.

In the afternoon they added a cup of sugar to each cup of juice and boiled them together until the mixture would fall two drops together from a spoon. Then the jelly was done. They put it in glass jars and covered the jars. These three drawings show how the jelly was made.

Cottage cheese for the cheese and jelly sandwiches was made by other boys and girls. It took longer to make than the apple jelly did. To make cottage cheese, milk has to sour and get thick. Bacteria in the milk will cause it to turn sour. The boys and girls who made the cheese brought milk three days before the lunch. They poured the milk into bowls and set it in a warm, clean, safe place on the kitchen table. They covered the bowls carefully.

The day before the lunch they put the sour and thickened milk into a pan and heated it to lukewarm temperature. They found out what lukewarm means by looking in the dictionary.

When the milk was lukewarm, it was poured into a bag over a pan and left to drip. A clear watery part of the milk dripped into the pan. A part of the milk had become somewhat solid. It stayed in the bag. It was cottage cheese. Its makers turned it into a clean bowl after the watery part had stopped dripping from it. They set the bowl aside until the next morning.

These three pictures show how to make cottage cheese from soured and thickened milk.

Early on the morning set for lunch in the classroom, committees did all these jobs:
1. Washed the leaves of lettuce and parsley
2. Boiled eggs hard and mixed them with chopped parsley when they were cold
3. Sliced the whole wheat bread and spread butter on the slices

158

Then other committees did these jobs:

1. Opened the cans of tuna fish, mixed the fish with salad dressing, and spread the mixture on slices of bread for the sandwiches

2. Spread the egg and chopped parsley on slices of bread for the sandwiches

3. Made the cottage cheese and jelly sandwiches

These committees wrapped the sandwiches in clean, wet towels to keep them cool and fresh.

When it was nearly lunch time, a small committee was left in the room to set the tables and heat the vegetable soup. The others went to the library.

This picture shows the hot vegetable soup being prepared.

The boys and girls on the committee are just about ready to set the tables.

Any meal should be served attractively. People should have interesting things to talk about. What is attractive in the way this lunch is served? If you were interested in science you might talk about science at lunch. That is what the boys and girls and Miss Hall did while they were eating this lunch.

Look back over this story of how they got ready for their lunch. In how many ways did they use what they knew about science? Make a chart to show the ways. Which of the seven basic foods were served?

Earth, Moon, and Sun

Look around You

Stand in a park or in a field some day and look around you. Wind may be blowing and moving the leaves and smoke. Cars may go whizzing by. Birds and insects and other animals may move around you. Airplanes and clouds may move across the sky. If it is early morning, the sun may seem to rise. You and the ground and buildings about you do not seem to be moving.

"When I stand still and look across the land or across lakes and seas, I know how human beings of long ago thought about the earth," Jack said. "It was a place that stretched about them, as far as they could see or go. It was sometimes rough land and sometimes smooth land. It did not seem to be moving."

"It seems that way to me now," Susan said. "I know it is not that way, but it seems so to me."

"The sun and the moon seem to move across the sky," Jane said. "I have watched them rise in the east and move up, up, up the sky. The direction of the shadows they make changes just as the direction of shadows change when you move a light in a room."

"It is easy to believe that the earth is flat," Sam said. "Sometimes you can see it stretching away before you for mile after mile."

"At the seashore I began to understand how people who were curious could see that the earth might be round," Mary said. "I have watched ships coming in. Far away I sometimes would see a tiny speck on the sea. Then as the ship came closer and closer to shore it became taller and taller."

This is a drawing that Mary made. It shows how ships seem to become taller and taller as they come nearer to shore.

"At first men made ships that could go only a small distance from shore," Tom said. "Then they made larger ships and learned how to manage many sails on a large ship. They went farther and farther away from shore."

"Columbus was one of the men who said that if a ship would set out and always sail west it would come back to its starting place," Sam said. "If they found out that what Columbus said was true, they would know that the earth was not flat but round."

"Old maps showed the earth as flat," Jane said. "I have been looking at one of them in this book of history. No one had made a globe in the time of Columbus because a globe shows that the earth is round. This old map is interesting. No one knew that there was an America when this map was made."

THE KNOWN WORLD - 330 B.C.

A globe is a small round object to show what the earth looks like. A globe is a model of the earth. This is a small globe that does not cost much. It shows that the earth is round. It shows where land and water are on the surface of the earth. It is different from the old map of a flat earth.

"Our globe is interesting, too," Jack said. "It shows the earth as men know it today. If I hold a light away from it in a dark room, I can understand day and night."

"You have to know something more about the earth than that it is round to understand day and night," Sam said.

"What else do you have to know?" asked Betty.

"If you walk around a globe or any round ball with a flashlight or any bright light, you can show that one half of the globe is light while the other half is dark," Sam said. "That does not help much in understanding day and night. If you walk around the globe with the bright light, you are doing what the sun would do if it moved around the earth. The sun does not move around the earth. The earth turns. Hold the light still and turn the globe. As you turn the globe, the light touches new parts of it. Darkness follows the light on the globe."

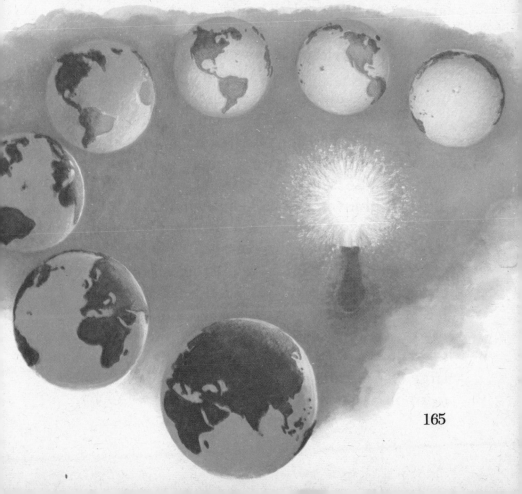

"How do you know that the earth turns?" Jane asked. "You see shadows change their direction, but they would do it if the sun moved and the earth stayed still."

"Astronomers are scientists who study the stars," Sam said. "Anyone who has seen stars overhead at night wonders about them. I do, at least, and astronomers do, too. How far away are the stars? What gives the stars light? Do the stars move around the earth as they seem to do? Are there some stars that can be seen every night? Astronomers were curious about the stars and the sun and the moon. They began to make guesses about them."

"When a telescope was invented, astronomers could see more," Miss Hall said. "Then they could prove that many guesses were true."

"I am not an astronomer," Jane said, "and I suppose I will never be one. I cannot prove that the earth turns to make day and night, but I am sure it does because astronomers say it does. They have all kinds of inventions to help them find out. I have made a trip to a place where astronomers study the stars. It is called an observatory."

"A telescope is like a magnifying glass and a microscope in one way," Jack said. "It helps us see better, but a magnifying glass and a microscope are used to help us see tiny objects that are near by. A telescope or field glasses are used to help us see large objects that are far away. Telescopes are used in an observatory."

"If you ever have a chance to look through a telescope be sure to do it," Sam said. "I went to an observatory one night last summer when the sky was clear. I looked through the telescopes there. It was easy to see the moon, stars, and planets."

This is an observatory. The round roof on the building can be opened, and a large telescope can be pointed through the opening. Everyone is curious about the stars, the planets, and the moon. Many inventions have been made to help people explain what they see in the sky. Observing the stars has been helpful. Observing the stars helped the first sailors to guide their ships. Observing the stars helps airplane pilots keep their airplanes going in the right direction. Observing the stars can help anyone find his way if he knows the direction he wants to go.

The Direction the Earth Turns

"Most of us believe that the earth turns, because scientists can prove that it does," Miss Hall said. "We can find out for ourselves the direction in which the earth turns and how long it takes to turn all the way around."

This is the way to find out the direction in which the earth turns.

An Experiment

1. What We Want to Find Out

   In which direction does the earth turn?

2. What We Need for the Experiment

   A globe or a large round ball. A bright light or flashlight. Some pins.

3. What We Do

   We stick pins in several places on the large round ball or on an old globe.

   We shine the light on the globe.

   We turn the ball or globe first in one direction and then in another, keeping the light in a fixed place.

4. What We Find Out

   We know that East is the name given to the direction where the sun is seen in the early morning.

   West is the direction where the sun is seen in the late afternoon.

   Shadows fall away from the light that makes them. Does the earth turn toward the East or toward the West? Did we turn the ball or globe from left to right or from right to left? Why must you ask, "In what direction were you facing?" before you can answer the question about turning the globe from left to right?

In how many hours does the earth turn all the way around? That is the number of hours in a day, for a day is the amount of time it takes the earth to turn all the way around. One part of a day is light. One part of the day is dark. What do we call the light part of a day? What do we call the dark part of a day? How can we find out just how long the earth took to turn all the way around?

The sun stays in its position while the earth turns all the way around. The earth has another motion, too. It goes around the sun.

"Most of us will have to believe that the earth goes around the sun, because scientists tell us it is true," Miss Hall said. "We can do some things to show what that motion of the earth is like."

Let one person stand in the center of a large circle. If a light is held by the person, it will be more like the sun. Let another person hold a globe and walk all the way around the sun, keeping on the line that makes the circle. This will be more like the earth going around the sun.

Astronomers know that the sun is a great, hot and glowing ball. Light rays go in all directions from it. Heat also goes out in all directions from the sun. Some of the light rays and heat from the sun reach the earth.

As the earth moves around the sun, it is rotating also. To rotate means to spin like a top. Because the earth turns all the way around every day or every twenty-four hours, we say it rotates.

When the earth goes around the sun we say it revolves. The animals on a merry-go-round revolve around the pole in the center. The earth revolves around the sun in one year. How many days are there in a year? Astronomers can mark on a sky map where the sun is on any day in a year. When it is in the same place again, a whole year has passed. How many seasons have passed while the earth revolves around the sun?

The moon revolves around the earth as the earth revolves around the sun. The moon is far away from the earth and so is the sun, but the sun is almost four hundred times as far away as the moon is. This is a drawing to show the moon revolving around the earth while the earth and the moon revolve around the sun. The dotted lines show the paths they follow.

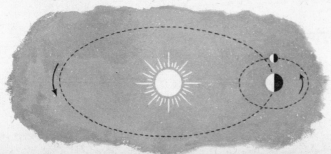

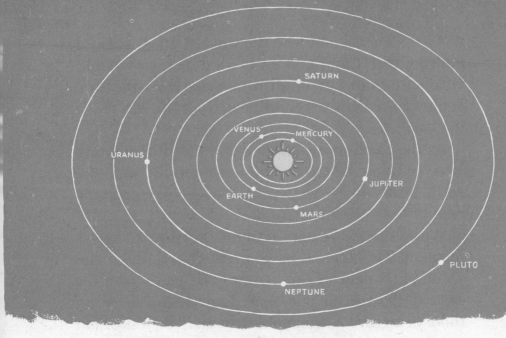

Our Solar System

The earth is a planet. Planets are large bodies like the earth that revolve around the sun. A sun, with the planets and all the smaller objects like moons that revolve about it, is called a solar system.

The sun is the center of our solar system. The earth revolves about the sun in a great path that is almost like a circle. The earth is only one of the planets of the sun. The planets of our sun are Mercury, Venus, Earth, Mars, Jupiter, Saturn, Uranus, Neptune, and Pluto. How many planets does our sun have?

This is a drawing to show our solar system. The sun is in the center. The sun's planets revolve about it.

172

The sun gives light and heat to the earth. It gives light and heat to its other planets. The sun is the only part of our solar system that is glowing with heat and light. We can see the sun. Can we see its planets? We live on the earth and we can see only a small part of it at a time. We also can see Mercury, Venus, Mars, Jupiter, and Saturn on a clear night when they are in the part of the sky at which we can look. The people who have very good eyes may be able to see Uranus. Neptune and Pluto are too far away to be seen without a telescope.

To us the planets of our sun look like stars in the sky, but they are not stars, for a star is a sun. Stars shine because of their own heat. They seem to twinkle. The planets and the moon shine because they reflect light from the sun. They shine with a steady light. They usually look brighter than the stars.

A good way to show reflected light is to turn a flashlight upon a large ball in a dark room. The side of the ball toward the flashlight reflects light. The reflected rays of light from the ball reach our eyes. We can see the ball. That is the way we see the moon and the planets of our sun.

The Universe

Our solar system is only a small part of the universe. Our solar system is made up of the sun at its center and the planets and some smaller objects that revolve about the sun. The moon revolves about the earth as the earth and the eight other planets revolve about the sun. Some of the other planets have moons, too. The moons that revolve about the planets are a part of our solar system.

Go outside on any clear night. Look into the sky. You may see the moon. You may see some of the planets. You are sure to see more stars than you can count.

Every star you see is a sun that is glowing with its own light and heat. Our sun would look like a star to a living thing with eyes like ours on a planet in another solar system. A star is too far away for its heat to reach you, but its light has reached you when you see it. Light from anything you can see reaches you. It may be reflected light. It may come to you from the object itself. Light comes to you from a glowing electric light. It is reflected to you from the other objects in a room.

Are there living things on the other planets in our solar system? Some astronomers think there may be plants living on the planet Mars. Are there living things on the other planets that may be revolving about other suns in the universe? No one knows the answers to those questions.

Star Pictures

Many people enjoy looking at the stars. They see pictures that the stars make in the sky. One of the star pictures that nearly everyone knows is the Big Dipper or the Great Bear. Different star pictures appear in the sky at different times of the year.

This is the star picture that is called Orion. According to an old myth, Orion was a famous hunter. He was changed into a star picture or constellation. His dog, Sirius, is still following him. People who wondered about the universe long ago saw the picture the stars made in the sky, and they made up the story about Orion.

Constellation means stars that appear to be placed to make a picture. Look toward the south, halfway up the sky, at about eight o'clock on a clear night in February. You will see Orion and Sirius. The stars that make the picture are billions and billions of miles apart. They only appear to be near enough together to make a picture.

ORION

175

Many stories about constellations are myths. An old myth tells the story of Cassiopeia. You can read about her in a book of myths. Cassiopeia was a queen. The constellation that is named for her is really her chair. It can always be seen on a clear night in the sky toward the north.

The North Star is a star that always seems to be in the same place in the sky. The two stars that make the front of the bowl of the Big Dipper point toward the North Star.

Cassiopeia's Chair is about as far from the North Star as the Big Dipper is. It is always on the other side from the Big Dipper. To most people, Cassiopeia's Chair looks more like a flattened letter W or M than like a chair.

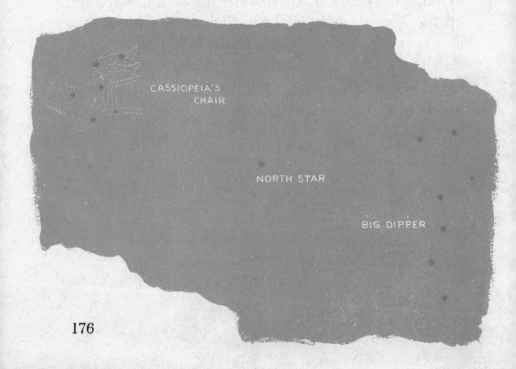

A Star Map

The Swan is a constellation that is in the Milky Way. This Star Map shows you how to find a constellation in the sky. You can practice doing it and perhaps you will find the Big Dipper, the North Star, Orion and his dog, Cassiopeia's Chair, and the Swan. On any clear, dark night you can see some of the Milky Way without using a star map.

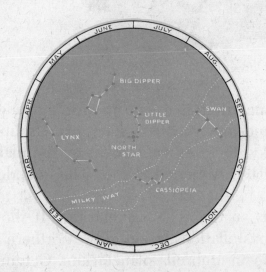

STAR MAP OF THE NORTHERN SKY

To use this map, face toward the north.

Find the name of this month on the edge of the star map.

Hold the name of the month at the top and over your head.

Make your observation at about eight o'clock. Find the Big Dipper first. Then find the other constellations you want to see.

177

A planetarium is a machine for showing the positions and movements of stars, planets, and moons in the sky. Pictures are thrown by the planetarium onto a large rounded dome. The rounded dome seems to be the sky.

This is an umbrella planetarium. It shows some of the constellations found in the northern sky. You can make an umbrella planetarium. Get an old umbrella with no handle. Cut circles of various sizes to be the stars. Stick the circles to the umbrella cloth to make the figures of the constellation. The North Star is located where the rod is fastened to the cloth. A small globe of the earth is placed where the handle of the umbrella would be. The northern sky constellations turn about the North Star. By turning the umbrella, you will be able to show this.

178

What Keeps the Earth, Moon, Planets, and Sun in Their Places?

"I believe what the astronomers say is true about the motion of the earth and the moon," one of the girls in the classroom said, "but why does the moon not move away from its path around the earth? Why do the earth and the other planets not move away from their paths around the sun?"

"Something must hold them in place," Dave said. "It must be something like what holds this ball in its path when I swing it around my head."

Dave swung a ball on the end of a string around his head. The ball stayed in its path.

"Anyone knows that no string holds the earth to the sun or the moon to the earth," Sam said. "The thing that holds the earth in its path around the sun only does what the string does. It is something that pulls. It is the pull of gravity."

179

A Balancing Toy

"Look," Tom said. "I have something to show how gravity works. It is a balancing toy. No matter how you set it down, it will turn head up. Watch it."

Tom set the balancing toy on its head. It turned its head up. He set it on one side and then on another side. The balancing toy always turned head up.

"Why does it always turn head up?" asked Mary.

"You can see how it is made," Tom said. "It has lead in this round bottom part. That makes the bottom part heavier. More weight is in the bottom. The pull of gravity there is more than on the head. The round bottom lets the toy turn in any direction. Gravity pulls the heaviest part more, and so the toy balances with its head up."

"I think I can help explain the pull of gravity," Miss Hall said. "If anything is heavier than air it falls to the earth, if it can. Throw a ball into the air. It goes up and then falls back to the earth. An airplane will fall to the earth if its engine stops working and its wings and tail do not keep it up long enough for the engine to start working again.

"Even air stays close to the earth for it has weight. The earth pulls everything as near to its center as it can. We say it is the force of gravity that pulls objects to the earth. The heaviest part of any object is pulled closest to the center of the earth, if the object can turn over. That is why the balancing toy always turns head up. Its bottom is heavier than its head."

Why are ink bottles and paste jars made with a heavy part at the bottom? How can people stay on the other side of the earth? Why does water not run back from the sea to the land?

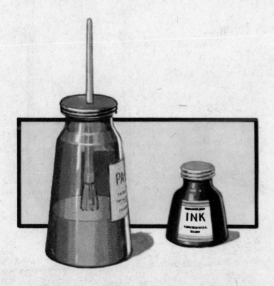

Water Level

Fasten a piece of rubber tubing about two feet long to the stem of a glass funnel. To the other end of the rubber tubing fasten a piece of glass tubing and pour some water into the funnel. Hold the funnel and glass tube in one hand.

Raise the funnel a little and observe what happens to the water in the glass tube. Lower the funnel, and observe what happens to the water in the glass tube.

Water is a liquid. As the funnel is raised or lowered, the pull of gravity causes the water in the funnel or glass tube to flow until a balance is made. We say that water "seeks" its own level.

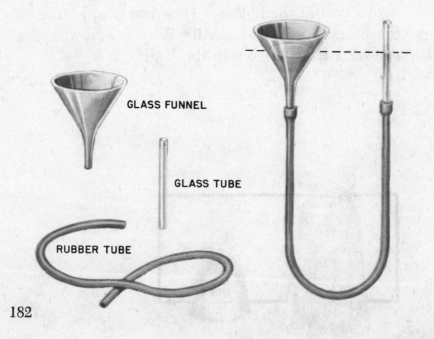

GLASS FUNNEL

GLASS TUBE

RUBBER TUBE

182

Sizes and Distances of Earth, Moon, and Sun

The sun and the moon look small to us. That is because they are so far away. The distance through the sun at its center is one hundred nine times the distance through the earth. The distance through the earth is four times the distance through the moon. No drawing could be made in a book to show the moon, the earth, and the sun side by side if the true distances through each were shown.

Let a pea seed be the earth. A rubber balloon that can be blown up to be two feet through its center would be the sun. A pinhead would be about the right size for the moon. You can see how hard it would be to make true drawings to show the sizes of each of them.

You have drawn pictures of many kinds. How do you show a car, a horse, a house, or the sun in the background if you want to put yourself looking at an ant near the front of the picture? Do objects look smaller the farther away they are? Why does an airplane high up in the sky look small?

183

Astronomers know that the sun is an enormous object that is an enormous distance away from the earth and that has an enormously high temperature. We can believe what they tell us, for they have invented instruments to help them measure the size and the temperature of the sun. We can find out for ourselves some things about the heat and light that the earth receives from the sun.

Suppose an electric light bulb is the sun. An object the size of a pinhead would be the size of the earth if the sun were the size of an electric light bulb. If you place the pinhead about eight feet away from the electric light bulb, that would represent the earth and the sun in something like their true positions in the universe.

Suppose the pinhead at the bottom of this page is the earth and the electric light bulb at the top of the next page is the sun and that the distance between them is about eight feet.

 EARTH

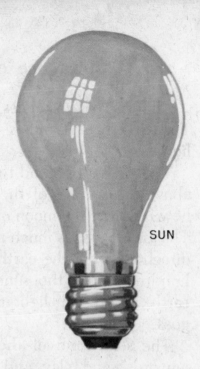

SUN

Even if the electric light bulb were enormously hot, the pinhead would get only a small amount of heat from it. Even if the electric light bulb were enormously bright, the pinhead would get only a small amount of all the light it sends out.

Where would all the heat and the light rays from the electric light bulb in a room go? Would some of the heat and the light rays fall on the pinhead that was about eight feet away?

Where would all the heat and the light rays from the sun go? Would some of them fall on the earth that was about 93 million miles away from the sun? If any planet was nearer the sun than the earth is, would it get more heat and more light rays from the sun than the earth does?

Substance of the Earth

All forms of substances can be found on the earth. The air is gas. Land is solid. Water and oils are liquids.

The air is all around the earth. It does not go far above the surface of the earth if you think about how far away the moon or the sun is from the earth. The air may go as much as five hundred miles in all directions from the earth. The moon is about two hundred forty thousand miles away from the earth. The air gets lighter in weight the higher up it goes.

The solid land of the earth is made of rocks, minerals, sand, clay, and decayed plant and animal materials. Rocks and minerals are the hard solid substances of which the parts of the earth are made. The highest mountains are not so much as six miles above the level of the sea.

Water in seas, lakes, and oceans has filled low places on the surface of the earth. The deepest part of the ocean bottom is not quite seven miles deep. This is somewhat lower than the top of the highest mountain is high. What is the highest mountain on the earth?

No one knows for sure what is in the center of the earth. The greatest depth to which anyone has gone into the earth is only a little more than a mile. It is about four thousand miles from sea level to the center of the earth.

The Earth's Surface

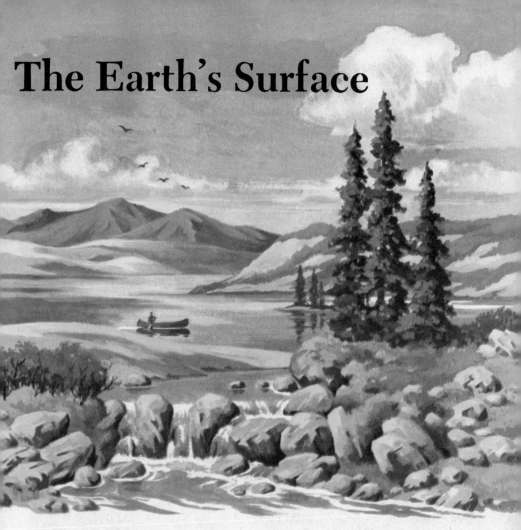

Changes of the Earth's Surface

Some of the surface of the earth is land and some is water. Water helps make changes in land. The land is the part of the earth's surface where people usually make their homes and where the plants of farms and gardens grow. The land of the earth's surface may be rough or it may be smooth.

187

Minerals

Many of the boys and girls had seen the collection of minerals in their school. This is the collection of minerals. The names are below the different minerals.

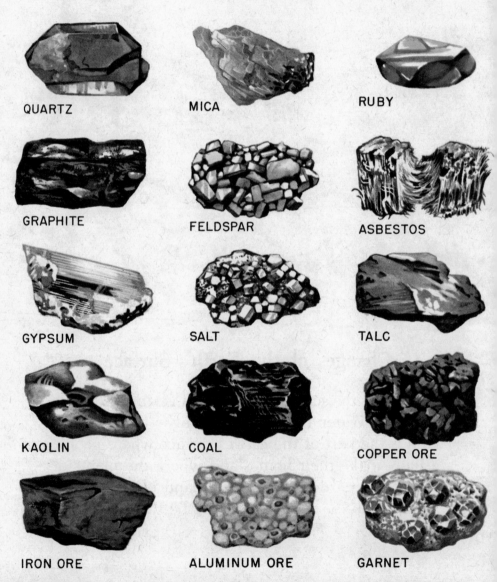

QUARTZ

MICA

RUBY

GRAPHITE

FELDSPAR

ASBESTOS

GYPSUM

SALT

TALC

KAOLIN

COAL

COPPER ORE

IRON ORE

ALUMINUM ORE

GARNET

While the boys and girls of the class had been looking at the collection of minerals, they had found out that some gems are minerals. Rubies, diamonds, opals, and all birthstones are gems. They are all minerals.

Quartz is the most common mineral in the world. It may be clear in color. It may be smoky, milky, or rosy in color. It is a hard mineral that will scratch glass. It cannot be scratched with a knife. Its form is interesting.

Mica is a common mineral. It reflects light well. It can be split into thin layers. The thin layers let light come through. Because it will not burn, thin layers of mica are often used in stoves to let light out into the room. Mica is sometimes called isinglass. It is very soft and can be easily scratched by a knife.

Kaolin is white clay that is used in making pottery. It is a mineral that melts at very high temperatures.

Asbestos is a mineral that will not burn. It can be picked apart as cotton can be picked apart. How is asbestos often used?

Plaster of Paris comes from a mineral that is named gypsum. That mineral is in the collection of minerals that the boys and girls had seen in their school.

Talc is a soft mineral. It is used in making talcum powder.

Graphite is the mineral from which the lead in pencils is made.

Iron, copper, and aluminum are all minerals. They come from iron ore, copper ore, and aluminum ore.

Knowing the names of some of the common minerals will help you understand more about the surface of the earth.

ASBESTOS

Crystals

"The quartz and feldspar have special forms," Jane said one day when she was looking at the exhibit of minerals in the Science Corner. "Some of the shiny quartz has six sides with pointed ends."

"They are crystals," Miss Hall said.

"We have examined snow crystals under a microscope," Jane said.

"We can make salt and sugar crystals," Miss Hall said. "We need sugar, salt, water, a magnifying glass, and dishes to hold the water with the salt or the sugar in it."

"We have everything we need," Jane said. "How do we make sugar and salt crystals?"

1. Making Salt Crystals

Pour five teaspoonfuls of warm water into a saucer. Add two teaspoonfuls of salt to it. Stir the salt into the water. The salt disappears in the water. We say it dissolves. When no more salt will dissolve in the water, lay a flat piece of paper in the saucer. Press it down to the bottom.

Then set the saucer of salty water in a place where it will not be moved. Let it stay there until all of the water evaporates. Salt crystals will be left on the paper in the bottom of the saucer. Where has the water gone? What form are the salt crystals?

2. Making Sugar Crystals

Dissolve as much sugar as you can in a drinking glass of hot water. When as much sugar as possible has been stirred into the hot water, pour some of the water into test tubes. Hang a cotton string in each test tube.

Set the test tubes in a place where they will not be moved. Let them stay there until all the water has evaporated. Sugar crystals will be left on the cotton string.

Examine the sugar crystals under the magnifying glass. What form are they? Are they the same form as the salt crystals?

If you have a collection of rock crystals, compare the salt and sugar crystals with them. You can compare them with pictures of rock crystals.

Sometimes you can buy rock candy. If you get a string of rock candy, you can compare it with the string of sugar crystals you have.

Many minerals make crystals when melted and then cooled. Quartz and feldspar are crystals that were made in that way. They were made in the earth when its surface was formed.

Calcite crystals, found in some of our limestone caves, have been formed by the evaporation of water.

Rocks or Stones

Rocks or stones are solid substances that are formed by nature in the earth. Rocks may be formed of only one mineral. Usually rocks are formed of many minerals that have been changed to become a solid substance.

Sand is formed of tiny pieces of rock and other solid substances.

Some rocks or stones are hard and some are soft. Some are colored and some are not colored. Some rocks are formed of other rocks that are held tightly together by other substances.

All the boys and girls in Miss Hall's class know that rocks do not grow. When they were talking about superstitions, they had learned that little rocks do not grow into big rocks. Some people say that rocks grow in a field. That is a superstition. Why would rocks appear in a field where they had not been seen before? What makes changes in the earth's surface? Did water help change the form of salt and sugar?

Making a Small Garden at School

Soon after Jack and Kate and the others had learned something about minerals and crystals, the class decided to make a small garden at school. Vegetables and flowers from the small garden could be used in many ways that the class talked about.

Everyone worked to prepare the ground for the small garden. It was hard work to clear the trash away and to get the soil ready for planting seeds and bulbs and for setting out plants. It was hard work to set out the plants that one of the boys had brought to school.

This is a picture of the class and Miss Hall working to get the soil ready. Many tools were used in the work. Who is using a lever? Who is using a wheel to help do work? How are some rocks being taken from the soil? Is the garden on a hillside?

Everyone was pleased when the hard work of preparing the small garden for seeds, bulbs, and plants was finished. Everyone was even more pleased when the seeds and bulbs had been put in the soil and when the small plants had been set out.

"Now if rain comes, we will have some flowers and vegetables to use as we wish," Jane said. She and the others had just come back to the classroom after the work had been finished.

That night a hard rain fell. The next morning this is what the boys and girls saw as they came to school.

"The rain washed our soil away," Jack said. "All our hard work was for nothing."

"We should have done something to keep our soil from washing away," Mary said.

"Much good soil in our community washes away when any hard rain comes," said the boy who had lived on a farm.

"It is a great waste to let soil wash away," Mary said. "We would not waste good pencils and paper."

"After a while all the good soil on the surface of the earth will be used up or washed away if people don't begin to build it up and use it wisely," Tom said. "I was looking at one of the books in the library the other day. Most of it was too hard for me to read, but I could look at pictures of land being washed away."

"I have a newspaper clipping that shows land that is being washed away," Kate said. "I thought I would put it in my Notebook for Science."

They all looked at the picture of the soil that had been allowed to wash away.

How Soil Is Made

"I suppose most people don't know how long it takes to make the soil that has been washed away so quickly," Miss Hall said.

"We know how quickly the soil in our school garden washed away last night," Susan said, "but how long did it take to make it?"

"I have read somewhere that it takes nature about five hundred years to make one inch of topsoil," Tom said.

"That is in the book you were looking at in the library," Miss Hall said. "I read it not long ago, and I am sure I saw something in it about how soil is made."

"May I get it now, and will you explain it?" Tom asked.

As soon as Tom returned from the library with the book, Miss Hall found the place where it told about how soil is made. She showed a picture of topsoil.

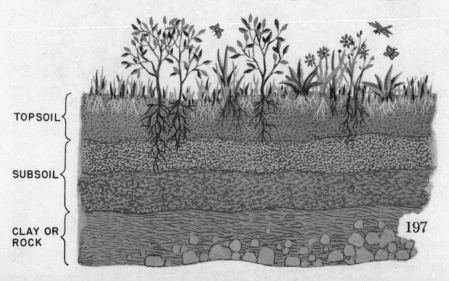

TOPSOIL

SUBSOIL

CLAY OR ROCK

197

"I'm not sure you will understand all that the book tells," Miss Hall said, "but I will try to tell you about how soil is made. Perhaps you can ask questions if I come to something that is too hard for you. This is the way I understand it.

"In the beginning there was no life on the earth. There were only land and water and air with the great burning sun shining down upon them. Volcanoes were active. Masses of land were pushed up by them."

"The land was bare rock. Sometimes whole masses of land sank below the waters. Geologists, who are people that study the way the earth was formed, say that millions and millions of years passed while the land rose and sank. Its bare rocks were cracked and changed during that long time.

"Changes in temperature caused the winds to blow then as they do now. You know also how on a freezing night the ice which is formed has sometimes cracked a pitcher or a bottle. Changes in temperature also cracked the rocks."

Our walks and roads are cracked this way, too. This is a picture of a road that was cracked by changes of temperature.

"Winds swept over the lands. They beat against the bare rocks and wore them into sand. They do it now, although we hardly see it done for it goes on slowly," Miss Hall went on.

"Waters, too, swept over the lands and wore them down and washed the bits of rock over the surface of the earth.

"It took millions and millions of years to do that, but little by little gravel and sand covered the rocks. Then plant life appeared. No one knows how the first plants began. After long periods of time, animal life appeared and again no one knows how it began.

"We do know what happens when heaps of dead plant and animal life are left on the ground. They decay. Bacteria, earthworms, and other animal forms help with their decay. Water, air, and changes of temperature help, and the decayed plants and animals are mixed with the sand and gravel.

"Ages went by after the first plants and animals appeared. Layer after layer of decayed plants and animals was added to the broken pieces of the rocks of which the bare earth was made.

"In that way the soil was made. It is the soil that makes the growth of plants and animals possible. The soil is something we should use wisely. It took a long, long time for it to be made."

Then Miss Hall stopped talking. "That was a long explanation," she said. "Do you understand the things I have told you?"

"Thank you, Miss Hall," Tom said. "I think I understand most of it now. I will try to read the book to myself to find out if I do."

"We don't all have time to read it and it might be too hard for some of us," Sam said. "We need to get to work again on the school garden. Perhaps Tom will ask questions about anything he does not understand. Then we can all talk together about soil. We can think about how it is made when we are working in it again."

The next day Tom said, "I understood almost everything about how soil is made when I read to myself what you had read, Miss Hall. You made most of it clear. The word humus was used in the book. You did not say exactly what humus is, but I saw a heap of it when we were working on the school garden one day. I think humus is the decayed animal and plant materials in the soil. Is that right, Miss Hall?"

"Yes," Miss Hall said. "That is right."

"I think I understand what the book told about changes that air, water, weather, plants, and animals make in the surface of the earth," Tom said. "They all helped to break up the bare rocks of the earth. They help do it now."

"I know how air in motion helps change the surface of the earth," Mary said. "Air in motion is wind. Wind blows sand into great heaps at the seashore. The great heaps of sand at the seashore are called sand dunes."

"Wind blows across plains and carries soil away," Jane said. "It changes some farms so much that people cannot live on them."

"If sand blows against stones, the stones will be worn away after many years," Susan said. "This is a picture of the way sand has been blown against an old building of stone and has worn it away."

Susan showed a picture of an old, old building. Everyone could see how sand was blowing and how the stone of the old building was worn.

"I can show you how human beings help wear stones away if you will come and look at the front steps of our school building," Jack said.

"Animals that walk over a stone year after year wear the stone away," said the boy who had lived on a farm. "I have seen deep paths worn in rocks by cows."

"Men sometimes take great heaps of stone away," Tom said. "I have watched them do it."

These are pictures that some of the boys and girls made to show other ways that animals and men have made changes in the surface of the earth.

"We know how water acts upon bare rocks and washes parts of them away if we have seen a stream running over stones," Jack said.

"I have seen a rock that was cracked by ice," Mary said.

"I am sure that you know that roots sometimes crack rocks wide open," Miss Hall said. "Air, water, animals, plants, and changes in temperature break or wear away rocks. They crack them open and then break them into smaller pieces, too. The small pieces of rocks are a part of the topsoil of the earth. Under the topsoil are more rocks that may be cracked and broken until they also become a part of the soil."

"Thank you, Miss Hall," Tom said. "I begin to understand it better."

"This is something I did not say," Miss Hall said. "It is that rocks contain minerals and that plants and animals need minerals for growth. I am sure you know that."

The boys and girls all nodded their heads to say that they did. Miss Hall went on explaining. "The animals in the soil help change the minerals in the rocks so that plants can use them. All kinds of animals and plants make changes in the minerals in the soil."

Tom nodded his head again.

"I begin to see what it all means," Tom said. "Rocks contain minerals. First of all the rocks had to be broken, and then the minerals could be dissolved in water so that the roots of plants could use them for food."

"Do you know how water gets down into the soil?" Miss Hall asked.

Tom thought for a minute. "I think so," he said. "It goes down cracks in the rocks. It goes down holes which roots of plants have made in the soil. It goes down holes which earthworms and other animals make in the soil."

"Then the minerals in the water are washed down into the soil through the holes that animals, roots, and water have made. Is that right, Miss Hall?" asked Charles.

"Yes, that is right, Charles," said Miss Hall.

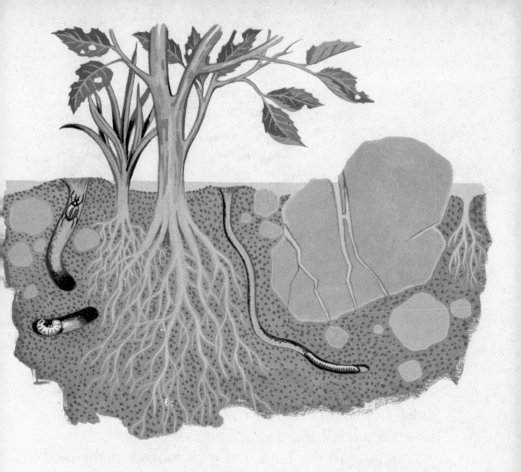

"Animals and plants help in making soil. "They also help make it good soil," said Charles. "I never thought much about that before."

"When we put fertilizer on the school garden, I read on the bag what was in the fertilizer. "I'll show you," Tom said.

Tom went out of the room. He soon came back with an empty fertilizer bag.

"Be careful, Tom," Susan said. "A schoolroom floor does not need fertilizer scattered over it."

Tom spread a newspaper under the fertilizer bag. "Look," he said. "Now where do you suppose all those minerals came from?" he asked.

Tom and all the boys and girls looked at the list of minerals on the fertilizer bag.

"From the rocks of the earth and from the air," Jack said. "When the rocks were broken, air and water could combine with the minerals and make part of the soil."

"The minerals are there for plants to feed upon," Miss Hall said.

"If the soil which contains them washes away, the plants have no food," Tom said. "I know that. Then if plants have no food, animals have no food. Rich soil is necessary for life upon the earth."

"If we do not use the richness of the soil wisely, we will lack food," Jane said. "We have learned how all living things depend on each other. We know now that they also need water, soil, air, and sunshine."

Tom had been looking at the names of the chemicals on the fertilizer bag. "We spread all those chemicals on the school garden," he said. "They must be important for making soil rich."

"They are," Miss Hall said, "and so are many other minerals. Farmers spend many millions of dollars every year to add fertilizer to soil that needs richness to produce good crops."

"It cost money to buy fertilizer to put on our school garden," Mary said. "The rain washed the fertilizer away with the soil."

"We are planning to put fertilizer on our school garden again," Jack said. "In a few days we are going to work on the garden again."

Preventing Erosion

"We have done a good job of preventing erosion in our school garden," Jack said after the hard work on the ground had been done a second time. "Looking at plowed fields has showed us how dangerous it is for the soil in a field if rows of any crop are planted up and down the slopes of a hill. Soil will wash away in a heavy rain. Erosion is the wearing away of soil. We have no ditches that run downhill. We have made all the ditches in our garden go around the hill in a level line. That is one way to prevent erosion of the soil by water."

"Running water has power," Mary said. "It can turn a water wheel. Water can carry huge logs downstream. Flood water can even tear up trees and wash whole houses away. If water runs downhill, it will carry soil away. The rows of corn on a farm should never be made up and downhill."

"We have filled in gullies with rocks and trash to stop water from running through them fast," Charles said. "We have planted grass on the side of hills. The principal of our school says that rain won't wash our plants and bulbs away again."

"We are not going to leave any of the ground bare in winter if we can help it," Sam said. "If soil is left bare, there is nothing to prevent the rain from washing it away."

"You said that soil should be used wisely, Miss Hall," Harry said. "We are going to try to keep the soil we have in our school garden."

"If I ever live on a farm again, I will know more about soil and how to prevent erosion," said the boy who had lived on a farm.

"We all will," Kate said.

You probably know more about preventing erosion of soil than you did before you learned about planting rows around a hill, filling gullies with stones and trash, and not leaving soil bare in winter.

Which one of the fields in the picture below is safe from erosion?

Telling the Age of the Earth

"In our talks about how soil is made, we have said that the earth is millions of years old. How do we know that it is very, very old?" Kate asked.

"Geologists are scientists who study the earth," Sam said. "They can tell us about how old the earth is."

"Anyone can observe a few signs that tell that the earth is very old," Miss Hall said. "At Niagara Falls, the Niagara River falls over solid rock into a deep gorge. The falls have cut the gorge for seven miles through solid rock. Geologists or anyone who lives near the falls can observe how small an amount of rock is worn away in one year or ten years. Only a small amount is worn away each year. It would take a long, long time to cut a gorge seven miles long if only a few inches were worn away each year."

212

"This is a picture of the gorge or canyon that the Colorado River has cut into the surface of the earth," Jane said. "The canyon is two hundred seventeen miles long and from four to sixteen miles across at the top. It has been cut by the river. In the hundred or more years that men have known about it, the canyon has changed somewhat. How long do you suppose it has taken the river to cut a gorge like the Grand Canyon?"

"We could never guess how many years," Charles said. "Only someone who knew could say how long."

"No one can say exactly how long it has taken," Miss Hall said. "Geologists know it has been a long, long time and they have ways of finding out. They observe and experiment and compare one part of the earth with another. About all we can do is to believe them."

"We can wait for someone to find out more facts," Harry said.

You may be able to tell something about the age of the earth if you take a trip along a road that goes over a mountain. Beside the road you may see layers of rock. The layers of rock are sometimes bent in waves. How did the rock become bent? Melted rock pushing up from inside the earth may have caused the surface of the earth to bend. Perhaps long ago the land beside the road was bent in waves.

This is a picture of the side of a road that goes over a mountain. Observe the rocks. Have you seen rocks like these near your home? If you can find rocks or stones that show layers of rock, bring them to school to show the boys and girls in your class.

Sometimes you may see layers of rock with shells in them beside mountain roads. The shells are of animals that live in the ocean, but now you see them in layers of rock high above the level of the sea. How did the shells get into the layers of rock?

The layers of rock were once on the bottom of a sea. The sea animals died and their shells were left on the bottom of the sea. Deeper and deeper the layer of shells grew as time went on. Sand and mud were washed into the sea and covered the shells. The shells and sand and mud were cemented together to form rock. Then the bottom of the sea was pushed up by a great bending of the surface of the earth. How long did it take to do all that? Scientists know it took a long, long time. The earth is very, very old.

A Test of What You Know

Which of these are used to prevent waste of soil?
1. Planting a cover crop for winter
2. Cutting all trees and pulling out stumps
3. Plowing around the hill
4. Raking leaves and burning them
5. Plowing the soil in autumn
6. Filling in gullies with stones and trash

Which of these can you prove by an experiment?
1. The earth is very old
2. Running water has power
3. Wind has power
4. Crystals of sugar are cubes
5. Glass is not a mineral

What is the meaning of these words?
1. rock
2. level
3. erosion
4. fertilizer
5. mineral
6. decay
7. geologist
8. humus

Weather

Beginning a Study of Weather

One morning Charles brought a clipping from a newspaper. It was the weather report for that day. Everyone in the class read it.

WEATHER REPORT
Rain and high wind today. Rain tonight and tomorrow with high winds. Storm coming from southeast. Yesterday's temperature: High, 85; Low, 76.

"I heard the weather report over the radio this morning," Sam said. "The man who gave the report said that a real storm was coming. It is coming along the coast. Much damage is expected."

The wind was blowing hard. Before long rain began to fall. Both wind and rain kept on all day. Most of the boys and girls had brought raincoats and rain hats, but the trip home was not easy for any of them.

That night the storm struck. There were thunder, lightning, and high wind. The rain poured down for nearly a week.

Streams overflowed, covering highways and bridges so that people could not travel over them. Crops in the low lands were covered with water and ruined. Electric light poles were washed out. Electric lines broke, and the electricity went off. The dam at the water-pumping station was washed out. The people had only the water that they caught from the rain or brought from wells and streams. They boiled water before using it. The storm did as much damage as the radio reporter had said it might.

Because of the storm, Charles, Sam, and all the others in Miss Hall's classroom became interested in weather reports.

"We have kept weather charts," Mary said. "I think we should make a chart to show all the things we know now about weather."

This is the chart they made.

WHAT WE KNOW ABOUT WEATHER

1. We have many kinds of weather.

2. Sometimes days are sunny. Sometimes they are windy, rainy, foggy, or snowy.

3. Sometimes the sky is cloudy, and sometimes it is clear.

4. The weather changes often.

5. Sometimes we have many kinds of weather in one day.

6. Temperature means how hot or how cold anything is.

7. A thermometer is used to tell the temperature.

8. Some clothes keep us warmer than others do.

9. We cannot do much to change the weather.

10. We change our clothes to suit the weather.

11. Wind is air in motion.

12. Warm air is pushed up by colder air.

13. We can fill in these lines with the right word. Can you?

It is warmer in the _____ (sunlight, shade).

Fog is _____ (water, smoke).

Frost forms on the grass when it is _____ (warm, cold).

Water is changed to ice by _____ (heat, cold).

Clouds are _____ (water vapor, water).

Steam is _____ (water vapor, water).

After Mary and the others had made the chart of things they know about the weather, they made a list of questions about how weather reports are made.

"I want to know about thunder and lightning," Kate said.

"Thermometers are used to tell how hot or how cold anything is," Susan said. "They are instruments that men have invented to help them make records of changes in temperature. I want to know what other instruments are used in making records of the weather."

You can find the questions that Kate and Susan asked in the list of questions on the next page. You can add questions of your own to the list.

List of Questions

1. How do people know what kind of weather we will have?
2. How does the weather man find out about the weather?
3. What instruments are used to find out about the weather?
4. What do clouds tell about the weather?
5. What does the wind tell about weather?
6. How does the weather man tell people what weather to expect?
7. How does the Weather Bureau help people?
8. What makes thunder?
9. What makes lightning?
10. What makes climate?

A Weather Station

This is a weather station. Miss Hall and the boys and girls are making a trip to it to find answers to some of their questions. On top of the weather station is a weather vane to tell the wind direction.

220

Near the weather vane is another instrument. It shows the speed of the wind. It is like a pinwheel. The wind blows against the cups and makes them move. The faster the wind is blowing, the faster the cups will move around. As the cups move around, a record of the speed of the wind is made. The instrument is called a wind gauge.

The boys and girls saw the wind gauge as soon as they reached the flat roof of the weather station. They saw many other instruments used for making weather reports. One of these instruments was a rain gauge. It was placed so that it would catch rain when any rain fell.

In the small house that is on the flat roof of many weather stations, there are thermometers for measuring the temperature of the air. Why are the thermometers placed in a house with openings in its sides? Why do many weather stations have flat roofs?

A Rain Gauge

Tom and Susan made a rain gauge somewhat like the one on the roof of the weather station. It was not as good as the one they saw, but when they used it, it showed how much rain fell.

First they made a stand of wood. Then they nailed a stick upright to one end of the stand. Next they sawed several inches from a broken yardstick and nailed the piece of yardstick to the upright stick.

Then they got a glass jar with straight sides and a wide opening. They wired the jar to the stand near the yardstick. The rain gauge was ready for use. They put their rain gauge on a box in the school yard.

When they measured the rain that fell one day, the yardstick showed that one half inch of water was in the jar.

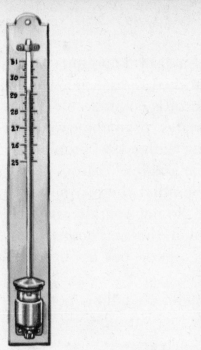

Barometers

This is a barometer. Jack and Miss Hall and the others saw one like it on their trip to the weather station. A barometer is used to measure the push of air. Cold air pushes warmer air away and takes its place. It is heavier than warmer air. If the push of the air becomes greater, the mercury in the barometer is higher. If the push becomes less, the mercury in the barometer is lower. The push of the air is called air pressure.

Changes in the reading on the barometer usually mean changes in the weather. If the reading on the barometer shows that the pressure is falling, a storm of some kind usually follows. If it shows that the pressure is rising, fair weather usually follows.

A barometer is a useful instrument to have at home. It can be studied to find out whether the air is clearing or a storm is coming.

A man who writes or makes weather reports could not get along without a barometer.

There are many kinds of barometers. Some of them contain liquids that the air pushes up or lets fall. Some of them do not contain any liquid. They measure the push of the air against a metal can whose sides move in or out as the air pressure changes.

This is a barometer that does not depend on a liquid. It is easy to carry around.

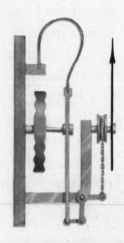

This is another way to make a simple barometer. It will show when the pressure of the air is rising or falling.

Bottle Barometer

Get a bottle and a one-hole rubber stopper which fits the bottle tightly. Push a glass tube into the hole of the rubber stopper. Put some colored paper in a glass of water until the water is colored. Pour the colored water into the bottle for a depth of an inch or two. The glass tube should almost reach the bottom when the stopper is placed in the bottle. The end of the tube must always be under the water. After pushing the stopper and glass tube into the bottle, blow through the tube. Do not blow too hard, or the water may be forced out of the tube. The water will rise part of the way up into the tube.

As the pressure of the air outside the bottle decreases, the air inside the bottle expands and pushes the water higher into the tube. In this barometer, the liquid rises as the air pressure outside of the bottle decreases. A falling of the liquid in the tube shows an increase in the pressure of the air. A rising of the liquid in the tube shows a decrease in air pressure. Fast temperature changes may change the liquid, too. A scale for noting the changes in the tube may be made by placing a stick containing markings back of the tube or by fastening a ruler to the tube.

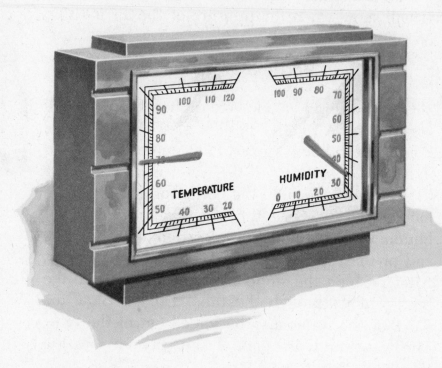

Tom told his class about an instrument at his home. "It shows the temperature on one measuring scale," he said. "On another measuring scale, it shows how much water vapor there is in the air. If the air is very dry, the reading on the scale is low. If the air is very moist, the reading is high. When the air is very moist and the thermometer begins to show that the air is getting cooler, we usually have rain. I do not know how the instrument is made, but it is interesting to watch. Sometimes by reading it carefully I can tell what kind of weather to expect."

Clouds

Susan and Tom and the other boys and girls in Miss Hall's class know about the evaporation of water. They know how water vapor becomes clouds and how clouds become rain.

When they came back from the trip to the weather station, they talked about observation of clouds to help in making a forecast of the weather. This is an experiment with the water cycle that they used to remind themselves of facts they already knew.

A Water Cycle

Get a tea kettle, a milk bottle, and a drinking glass. Place the tea kettle on the stove, and heat the water to boiling. Hold the mouth of the milk bottle over the spout of the tea kettle. Use the drinking glass to catch the water that drips from the bottle. If the milk bottle becomes too hot to hold, wet a cloth or towel in cold water and keep the bottle cool. This water cycle is much like the cycle in nature. Water, heat, water vapor, cooling, water again—that is the water cycle. Heat is necessary for evaporating water. Cooling must take place before water vapor turns into water.

This experiment may be used to show how water may be freed of other substances. Put some salt into the water in the tea kettle and catch some of the steam in the milk bottle. As soon as you get enough water in the glass to taste, see if it is salty.

Water Cycle Chart

A water cycle chart may be made on a large piece of cardboard. Puffy balls of cotton serve as clouds and may be pasted to the cardboard. A sun that gives heat for evaporation of water may be painted on the cardboard. Zig-zag strings can be used to show evaporation of the water.

The rain from the cloud may be shown by strings which are put through the cardboard.

A lake of water can be made by cutting out blue paper in the shape of the lake and pasting it on the cardboard.

Trees may be cut from pieces of cardboard and pasted in place. The land can be drawn or painted on the cardboard.

Why is this called a water cycle chart?

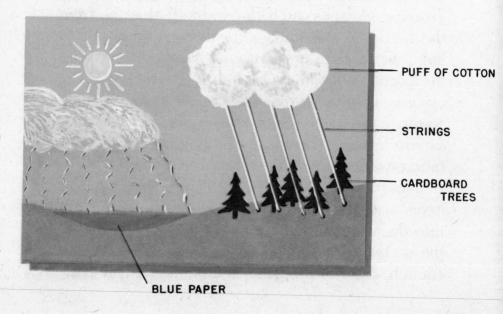

PUFF OF COTTON

STRINGS

CARDBOARD TREES

BLUE PAPER

After the trip to the weather station, the boys and girls and Miss Hall began to observe clouds more carefully. They found out that there are several kinds of clouds. Each kind has a meaning for the weather man.

1. Cumulus Clouds

Cumulus clouds are usually the sign of fair weather, but sometimes they are in the sky just before a rain. The name cumulus means a heap. Cumulus clouds are like piles of white cotton up in the sky. They are the kind of clouds that are most often seen in the sky. If they are in the sky on the opposite side from the sun, they are usually shining white. If they are on the same side of the sky with the sun, they look dark with white or golden edges.

2. Cirrus Clouds

Cirrus means curl or ringlet. Cirrus clouds are curly, white wisps of clouds. They are thin clouds and look like feathers of soft white down. They are made of ice crystals.

Cirrus clouds are always high up in the atmosphere. Most often when you see them they are traveling very fast across the sky. Sometimes you can see them high above cumulus clouds. They may be traveling in an opposite direction to that in which the cumulus clouds are traveling.

3. Nimbus Clouds

Nimbus is a word meaning cloud. This name has been given to clouds which produce rain. They often cover much of the sky. Nimbus clouds are usually gray in color. These clouds bring most of our rain and snow.

4. Stratus Clouds

Stratus means layer. Stratus clouds are layers of smooth, hazy, usually gray clouds. They form near the earth. These clouds are usually seen early in the morning and late in the afternoon. Their colors change as the sun shines behind them and through the open spaces.

Questions about Clouds

1. Why do the shapes of clouds change?
   a. If wind blew clouds, would their shape change?
   b. If the water in the clouds evaporated, would the shapes of clouds change?
2. Why do clouds disappear from the sky?
   a. Could wind blow clouds away?
   b. If the water in the clouds evaporated, would the clouds disappear?

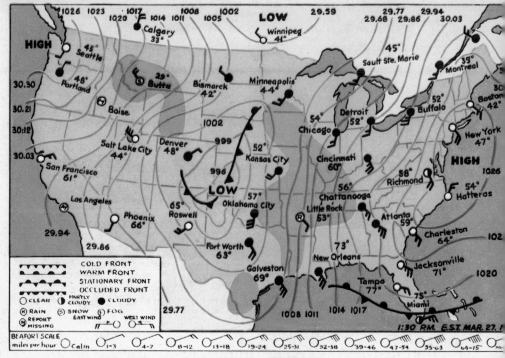

Weather Maps

Weather maps are made by using reports from many weather stations all over the United States and sometimes from all over the world. Look at the weather map on this page. It gives the temperature for all the weather stations that make reports. Numbers at the ends of the solid lines give the readings on barometers.

"Low" on the weather map means that the barometer shows low pressure of the air. That usually means that rain or snow or some kind of stormy weather is present. "High" on the weather map means that the barometer shows high pressure of the air. That usually means that fair weather is present.

The Weather Bureau

The Weather Bureau is a part of our government. The main office is in Washington, D. C. There are eight chief weather stations. They are in New York, Atlanta, Chicago, Fort Worth, Kansas City, Los Angeles, Seattle, and Anchorage, Alaska. There are over five thousand other smaller stations. At eight o'clock every morning and every evening, each of the smaller stations makes a report to the nearest one of the eight chief stations. They report on temperature, barometer reading, amount of rain or snow, direction of wind, speed of wind, kind of weather, and clouds. From the reports the eight chief stations make weather maps. The weather reports are printed in newspapers and given over the radio.

Thermometers, barometers, rain gauges, weather vanes, and wind gauges are some of the instruments used in weather stations for getting records. Sometimes balloons are sent high into the upper air with weather instruments fastened to them. Records are made on the instruments by weather conditions. When the balloons burst, the instruments come slowly back to earth by means of a parachute. The records on them are read. Some balloons have small radio sets which broadcast the weather conditions back to the weather station.

Weather maps and weather reports help fishermen, fruit growers, farmers, and many other people to make preparations for changes in weather.

Lightning and Thunder

"Anyone who is interested in clouds and weather will be curious about lightning and thunder," Miss Hall said.

"I saw a tree that lightning had struck last summer," Sam said. "I found out about lightning then. I know what causes it. Lightning is one kind of electricity. It is a spark of electricity jumping from one cloud to another or from a cloud to the ground."

"One day in winter I went across the rug in our living room to open the door," Jane said. "When I put out my hand to touch the metal door knob, I felt a spark of electricity."

"Sometimes you can hear the sparks of electricity crackle when you are combing your hair," Susan said.

"If you rub a plastic comb on your hair or on wool you can pick up pieces of paper with it," Jack said.

"If you rub a glass rod with a piece of silk, you can do the same thing," Sam said. "Rubbing the rod with silk gives the rod a charge of electricity. Friction does it."

"I suppose I gave myself a charge of electricity when I rubbed my shoes on the rug," Jane said.

Picking Up Paper with Your Pen

This is one way to give a charge of electricity to a substance. Try it with many substances.

Rub your fountain pen back and forth on woolen cloth. Then bring the fountain pen near some small bits of torn paper. The pieces of paper will jump to the fountain pen.

Rubbing the pen on the woolen cloth charges the pen with electricity. The bits of paper jump to the pen as the pen is brought near them. The paper is not charged with electricity. Some of the pieces of paper may jump to the pen and then fly off again. This happens as the paper becomes charged with electricity. Electric charges that are not alike attract each other. Electric charges that are alike repel each other. This experiment works best on a cold, dry day. The electricity is produced by rubbing one substance over another. It is produced by friction.

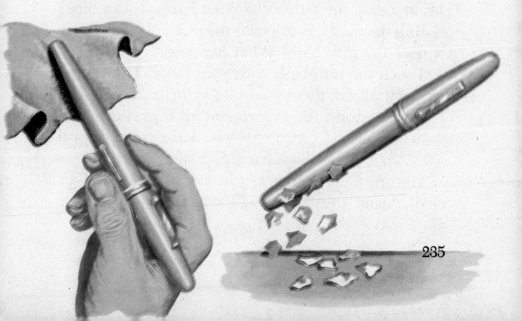

An Experiment

1. What You Want to Find Out
Are the charges of electricity alike if they are made in different substances by friction?

2. What You Need
Glass rod and piece of silk

Plastic comb and piece of wool

Small pith balls hung by silk threads from a wooden stick. (You can get pith from a stalk of corn. If you look around you, you may be able to find pith in stalks of other plants. You may also use two dry puffed wheat kernels instead of pith balls.)

3. What to Do
Rub the glass rod hard with the piece of silk. Bring it near the pith balls. What happens?

Rub the glass rod again with the piece of silk and bring it near the pith balls. What happens this time?

Rub the plastic comb with the piece of wool. Bring it near the pith balls. What happens?

Touch the pith balls with your hand. The charge of electricity in them goes into your hand.

Now perform the experiment all over, but begin with the plastic comb that you have rubbed hard with wool. What happens this time?

Try rubbing other substances with silk or wool. Some substances will not take a charge of electricity.

4. What You Find Out

Rubbing glass with silk gives the glass a charge of electricity, for the glass will attract substances such as pith balls and pieces of paper. If the pith balls touch the glass rod, they receive the same kind of charge of electricity from the glass rod. Then they fly away from the glass rod. We say they are repelled or kept away by the same kind of charge.

Rubbing the plastic comb with wool gives it a charge of electricity, and the comb will attract substances such as pith balls and pieces of paper. If the pith balls have a charge of electricity from the glass rod, will they be repelled by the comb? If they are attracted by it, they have another kind of charge of electricity.

If the pith balls had a strong charge of electricity in them and they could not fly to the plastic comb which also had a strong charge in it, what would happen? The same thing would happen that happened when Jane walked across the rug on a cold day and put out her hand toward the door knob.

In a thunder storm, currents of air blow about and break raindrops into fine spray. This movement gives a charge of electricity to clouds. The top part of a cloud may have one kind of charge in it, and the bottom part of the cloud may have a different kind of charge in it. One cloud may have one kind of charge of electricity in it, and another cloud may have a different kind of charge in it. The charges may become large enough to jump from one place to another. Clouds having different kinds of charges may come near enough for a spark to pass from one cloud to another. The spark may jump from one part of the cloud to another or even to the ground.

The huge spark of electricity is the lightning we see. Sometimes the spark divides and we can see it spreading out like the branches of a huge tree turned upside down.

Sparks of electricity from one cloud to another or from the bottom to the top of the same cloud do no harm. A spark from a cloud to the earth may be harmful. Trees are sometimes killed by being struck by lightning. A barn or house may be set on fire by lightning. These things seldom happen.

A spark of lightning is very hot. As it goes through the air from one place to another, it heats the air and causes it to expand very rapidly. Heat always causes substances to expand. If you have some books of science in your Science Corner, you can probably find some experiments to prove this.

When the spark of electricity heats the air and causes it to expand very quickly, it sets up waves in the air. The waves reach our ears and make a sound which we call thunder. The wave from the top of the spark reaches our ear first and then keeps on reaching it until the spark ends. This gives a rolling sound. Some of the sound may be reflected from clouds and that adds to the rolling. This is like the echo that is reflected from a building or mountainside.

Thunder may scare you, but it does no harm. Thunder follows lightning and is caused by rapidly expanding air that the electric spark has heated.

Why do we always see the lightning before we hear thunder? Sam says it is because light travels faster than sound. Which do you think travels faster? How can you find out?

Climate

"What is climate?" someone in Miss Hall's class-room asked.

The earth has many different kinds of climates. Some places on the surface of the earth have a warm, moist climate. Some of them have a hot, dry climate. Some have a cold, dry climate. Some have a cool, moist climate.

What is climate? Suppose you lived where most of the days in the summer were hot and dry. You would say that your climate in summer was hot and dry. Suppose most of the days in winter were cold and moist. You would say that your climate in winter was cold and moist. If it was warm and wet for most of the days where you live, you would say that you live in a warm, wet climate.

Weather is the day-to-day temperature, wind, rainfall, snowfall, sunshine, clouds, fog, sleet, and ice. Climate is the kind of weather a place may have for long stretches of time.

Eskimos live in a cold climate. What does that mean?

Mountains may keep cold winds from blowing upon a place, or they may be the cause of cold winds sweeping over a place on the earth. How would the sea affect climate?

What kind of climate does this place probably have for most of the year? What makes you think so?

In different places, the climate is different. What kind of climate does this place probably have for most of the year? What makes you think so?

241

Who Uses Reports on the Weather?

At the end of their study of weather, Charles and the others made up some stories and found pictures to show that they knew about many kinds of weather. The stories told about people who use weather reports. You can make reports to show other people who use weather reports.

1. SCHOOLS USE WEATHER REPORTS

If the caretaker of our school hears that cold weather is expected, he starts a fire in the furnace. He starts the fire in time for the furnace to become hot and for the heat to rise from the furnace into the classrooms.

If a weather report comes over the radio that a blizzard is expected at one o'clock, school is dismissed in time for the boys and girls to get home before the blizzard reaches their community. If a weather report about the coming of a blizzard reaches the homes before the boys and girls start to school, another report will probably come over the radio or the telephone that there will be no school that day.

2. FARMERS USE WEATHER REPORTS

If a farmer hears a report that rain will probably come in a few days, he hurries to put his cut hay into stacks or into the barn. What harm would rain cause to cut hay? Why does a stack protect hay? If a farmer hears that rain is expected, he hurries to plant seeds in the ground he has plowed. Why should seeds be put into the ground before a rain? If floods are expected, a farmer may see that protecting walls of earth around his low fields are built up.

3. FRUIT GROWERS USE WEATHER REPORTS

If a fruit grower hears that frost is expected, he may build fires that will make smoke to protect his orchard from frost. A gardener who hears that freezing weather is coming may cover his young plants.

243

4. AIRPLANE PILOTS USE WEATHER REPORTS

If an airplane pilot hears that a heavy fog is expected over the mountains where his plane must travel, he may keep the plane on the ground. He waits for a report that the weather is clearing. If a traveler wants to make a trip to a place that is in a storm's path, he will wait to make his trip until the storm has passed.

5. FISHERMEN USE WEATHER REPORTS

If fishermen hear a weather report that a storm is moving into their fishing grounds, they will keep their boats tied up near the shore. Reports of a bad storm at sea may cause ships to stay in the harbor until the storm has passed.

Ways of Travel

Crawling

Miss Hall and the boys and girls had formed a circle to talk about a snail and an earthworm that Kate had brought. They had just finished their stories about who uses weather reports.

"I was riding along to school on my bicycle," Kate said. "I was going slowly, for you know that it rained last night. The road was slippery, and I was being careful. Suddenly I saw this snail, and near by was this earthworm. I had a small box in my school bag for collecting anything that interested me."

"You brought them here faster than they could have come the way they travel," Charles said.

"How do snails and earthworms travel?" Harry asked.

"They crawl," Charles said. "If we put them on flat pieces of clear glass, we can see better how they do it."

Flat pieces of clear glass were brought from the Science Corner in the schoolroom. The snail was placed on one piece of glass and the earthworm on another piece.

The earthworm began to crawl on the piece of glass at once. "It pushes its head part forward," Susan said. "Then it pulls itself along. It extends itself and pulls itself together."

"The earthworm has muscles in its body," Jack said. "Its muscles seem to expand and to contract."

"The snail is extending its head from its shell," Jane said. "Now it is beginning to crawl. It extends itself and pulls itself together, too."

"I suppose anything that moves without feet uses muscles in its body to extend and then pull," Mary said. "The snail makes a sticky track when it crawls and I suppose that helps it hold on while it pulls."

"Snakes crawl but they can go faster than earthworms or snails," one of the boys said. "I have watched them moving. They have ridges on their bodies and can hold on to surfaces better while they pull themselves forward."

"They wriggle, too," Harry said. "That helps them push and pull. Snakes can run faster than I can."

"I have watched the snails and other animals in our aquarium travel," Jack said. "Fish have another way to travel."

Swimming

After they had looked at the fish moving about in the water, Sam said, "Fish have muscles in their bodies, too."

"They move their fins forward and then push against the water with them," Mary said. "That moves their bodies forward in the water."

"It is the way I move a boat forward in the water at the lake in the summer," Jane said. "I put one end of the oars forward in the water. I push on the other end. The boat moves forward."

"The oar on a boat is a kind of lever," Mary said. "I can show you how it is a lever."

Mary drew a picture to show what she meant. The end of the oar in the water is where the lever stays still. It is the fulcrum. Mary showed what she meant by a fulcrum by drawing another picture beside the first one.

"The fulcrum of a lever is the part that stays still. The weight is the part that moves, and the power is the force that makes the weight move," Mary said. "The boat with the person in it is the weight that moves. The force that makes the weight move is the pull given by the person who is rowing the boat."

FULCRUM

"When I swim, I move my hands and arms forward and pull against the water with my hands flat against it," Charles said. "My hand against the water is the fulcrum. I am the weight that moves. My muscles are the force. Sometimes I use my legs and feet as levers, too. Fish move their fins as I do my hands and arms."

"The fish have other fins to help them turn in the water," Jack said. "They can go up or down or to either side. They can even swim backward."

"Fish can swim faster than I can," Kate said. "I have tried to catch them in the water where we sometimes swim. They are gone before I can put my hand out."

"Swimming is a good way to travel if you live all the time in water the way fish do," Miss Hall said. "I have watched seals in a large aquarium in the city. They can move in almost any direction, and they go very fast."

"Seals and fish can swim. Snails and earthworms and snakes can crawl. I know another way I would like to travel," Harry said.

248

Flying

"If you look from our window, I think you can see the way Harry means," Tom said. "I think he means flying. I wish I could fly."

"Birds use their wings to fly through the air as fish use their fins to swim through the water," Susan said. "They have muscles in their bodies. I have seen the muscles on a chicken that Mother was preparing to cook. The muscles around a chicken's wing are strong. The muscles move the wings up and down. The wings are broad and push against the air. The chicken's body moves forward when it pulls. Chickens are birds."

"I know a bird that can swim and fly," Jack said. "What bird is it?"

"Ducks swim and fly. They walk and run, too," Sam said.

After they had observed the snail, the earthworm, the fish, and the bird, everyone sat down in the circle again.

"I know that animals move in many ways," Jack said. "Anyone knows it who has watched animals the way we have, but I am interested in the ways human beings move. I am not interested in how their muscles help them move their arms and legs, but in how they have invented ways to help them travel faster."

"I am more interested in airplanes than in any other way to travel," Sam said. "I have just pasted a picture of an airplane in my scrapbook. It can travel more than six hundred miles in one hour. It could go all the way around the world in less than two days if it could carry enough fuel to keep it going."

This is the picture of the airplane Sam showed.

That is the way the class began a study of how inventions have changed the ways men travel. They found out about the first airplane that would carry a man in the air. This is the story they wrote about it.

Success at Last

For a long, long time before the first airplane was made, people had tried and tried to find some way to fly. They could walk or hop or jump or run. They could wade or swim in water. They could ride on water or land.

Those ways of travel were not enough for them. They wanted to fly as birds do.

Many people watched birds flying through the air. They tried to find ways of flying, too. When the wind was blowing, they performed experiments with kites.

Then someone made a machine that would glide through the air as he had seen birds gliding through the air without moving their wings. That was a beginning, but it was not enough.

Success came at last as everyone knows very well. Someone made a machine that would leave the ground, fly through the air, and carry a man in it. The men who made that first airplane were Orville Wright and his brother Wilbur. Their last name can be seen upon some airplanes today.

Orville and Wilbur Wright lived in Dayton, Ohio. They liked machines, and they knew how to make many kinds of machines. When they were boys, they went about Dayton doing any kind of job they could find to earn money. When they grew older, they worked on machines and did other small jobs to help make a living. Always at night they read about machines, especially those that might fly. By day they used all the time they could to work on their flying machines. They made kites and watched them fly. They made gliders and tried to fly them when the wind was blowing.

How people laughed at them. When they were out trying to fly in their gliders, people came around to watch them. "Ho, ho, ho!" the people laughed. "Those Wright brothers will never make a flying machine that can carry a man. No one can."

Orville and Wilbur Wright decided to go away from Dayton, Ohio, and find another place to work. They wanted a place where there were not so many

252

people. It should be sandy also to give a soft place to land when they fell. It should have long slopes from hill tops and no trees. There should be wind most of the time. That place, they decided, was Kitty Hawk, North Carolina. Kitty Hawk is on the seashore where it is sandy.

Anyone who has been in Kitty Hawk, North Carolina, will know what a sand dune is. It is a hill made of sand that the wind blows here and there. Sometimes the sand dunes change their places almost overnight. There are sand dunes all around Kitty Hawk now.

There were sand dunes at Kitty Hawk when Orville and Wilbur Wright went there. Gliders could be taken to the top of high sand dunes. From there they could be started off. People would not get in the way for there were only a few people in Kitty Hawk in those days. There were few trees. It was a very good place for the Wright brothers to work.

How the Wright brothers worked with their gliders at Kitty Hawk! At last they learned how to make them do some of the things they wished. It must have been fun to see them on top of a high hill of sand trying to glide from it in their glider.

At last the work with gliders, the first part of the job, was finished. The brothers hurried home to Dayton, Ohio. There they made an engine and they put it on their glider.

Then they went back to Kitty Hawk. This time they wanted to try out a real flying machine. It would not have to make use of the wind to stay up as gliders did. It would have its engine, and that would make it go. At least that is what Orville and Wilbur Wright thought.

The day finally came for the glider with the engine upon it to be tried out. Out to the sand dunes went the Wright brothers, and they took the glider with its engine. Orville sat in the airplane. Would the machine fly?

Orville started the engine. The propeller went around and around. The airplane flew and it carried a man. Hurrah, hurrah! Success at last! That was on December 7, 1907. Not many people were there to see that first flight, but the Wright brothers are famous today.

The airplane did not fly far that first time, but others did after a while. Orville and Wilbur Wright had done a good job.

Up in the Air

"What makes a glider stay up in the air?" Charles asked. "It is made of wood or metal. Wood and metal are heavier than air. Why do they stay up in the air?"

"It is the way air pushes on the wings of the glider and the motion of wind that keep it up," Sam said. "If you tie a string to a piece of paper and pull it through the air, the paper will stay up. The paper won't stay up if you don't keep pulling."

"If you take a piece of paper in your hand and pull it through the air, the part that is not held will float up and down," Jane said. "Try it and find out."

"You have to run with a kite to get it to start up into the air," Jack said. "Then it will stay up in the air if the wind is blowing, but you have to be careful to tie the string to the kite in the right place."

"You must tie the string so that the wind can push up on the surface of the kite," Sam said.

The Push of Air

"I know that air pushes against any surface that moves against it," Charles said. "Will it push if the surface does not move?"

"I cannot feel it pushing against my hand if I don't move my hand," Kate said.

"We can perform some experiments to show that air pushes in all directions," Miss Hall said. "It would help us understand why airplanes and gliders stay up in the air only when they are moving or when the air is moving against them."

These are the experiments that they performed.

An Experiment

1. What You Want to Find Out

Does air hold water in a glass if the glass is turned upside down? Does it hold water in the glass if the glass is turned sideways? Does air seem to push against a surface from all directions?

2. What You Need

A drinking glass

A piece of cardboard large enough to cover the top of the drinking glass

Water enough to fill the drinking glass

3. What to Do

Take the glass and the water outside or to the sink.

Fill the drinking glass with water.

Hold the cardboard on top of the glass of water.

Hold the cardboard in place and turn the glass with the water in it upside down.

Take your hand carefully away from the cardboard.

If you turn the glass sideways carefully, you will find out something more about the direction from which air pushes.

Turn the glass in all directions.

4. What You Find Out

In what direction does air seem to press?

If the water were not in a glass, would the water stay up in the air?

When the glass of water with the cardboard over the opening is turned upside down, why does the air not press on the water from above and from the sides?

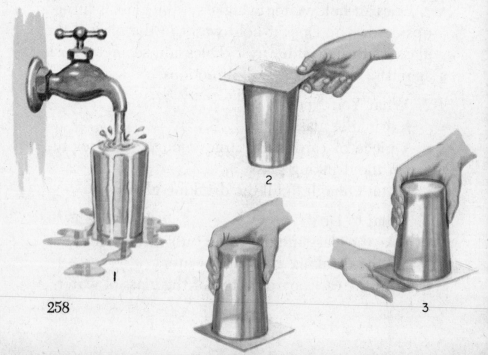

An Experiment with Air Pushing from Above

The last experiment showed that something held the cardboard over the opening when the glass was turned upside down. It showed that something held the cardboard in place when the glass full of water was turned sideways. What was the only thing that touched the cardboard after your hand was taken away? If you let a little air into the glass, will the cardboard hold the water in the glass? Try it and see if it does. This is another way to show that air pushes on any surface from above.

Sticking Coins to Glass

Get a piece of window glass or plate glass. Moisten several coins with water and press them close to the glass plate and they will stay there.

The coins are held in place by the push of the air. Moistening the coins with water causes them to fit flat against the glass plate. The air from between the coins and the glass plate is pushed out when you press them against the plate.

259

An Experiment to Show Air Pressure

This is another experiment to show that air pushes against a surface. Write it as an experiment after you try it.

It Pours and It Does Not

Get a milk bottle. Stretch a piece of thin cloth over the mouth of the bottle and fasten it with a rubber band. Fill the bottle with water by pouring the water through the cloth.

Turn the bottle upside down and the water does not pour out. Hold the bottle on its side over the sink and the water pours. Turn the bottle upside down again and the pouring stops.

Thin cloth has many small openings. A thick layer of water covers the openings and sticks to the cloth. The pressure of the air against the layer of water and the cloth holds the water in the bottle. As the bottle is turned on its side over the sink, the air enters the upper holes of the cloth and forces the water out.

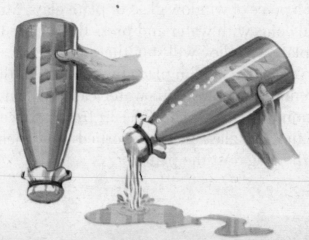

Motion and the Push of Air

"I see now that air pushes against surfaces from all directions," Charles said. "Moving an object like a piece of paper through the air will cause it to go up or down. I know also that if air moves against objects, they will move. I still do not know exactly why a glider stays up in the air or why an airplane does."

"My uncle was an aviator," said Jane. "This is the way he showed me what lifts and holds up an airplane." She folded about an inch of a sheet of paper as the picture shows. She placed the paper on a table and blew hard over the upper surface of the paper.

"Did you see the paper rise when I blew over it?" she asked. "Why did it rise?"

"Air under the paper pushed it up," Sam said. "The moving air over the top pushed down with less force than the air below pushed up. As long as the air keeps moving, the paper stays up."

A Glider Takes Off

The glider that Orville and Wilbur Wright used for their experiments at Kitty Hawk had curved surfaces to get the lift of air when it moved against the wind. It had wings and tail pieces, too. The tail piece of the glider had a rudder for guiding it. On each side of the rudder there were two flaps called elevators. The elevators could be moved up and down. Here are two drawings of the glider. One of them has the elevators raised. The other shows the elevators lowered.

If the elevators of the glider were raised, the glider went higher into the air. If the elevators were lowered the glider came closer to the ground. If the flap on one wing was raised and the flap on the other wing was kept straight, the glider turned toward the side with the flap raised. A man sat in the glider to raise or lower the flaps. If wind was blowing, the glider stayed up longer.

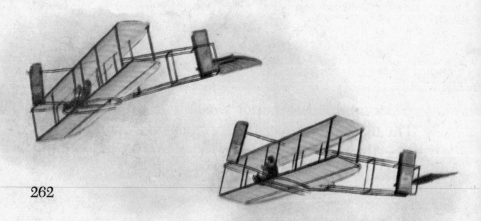

Inventions and Airplanes

"Airplanes today do not look much like the one that first carried a man through the air," Charles said.

"Inventors are working all the time to make better airplanes," Dave said. "They want airplanes that will go faster. They are making better and stronger engines all the time. They are finding new kinds of fuel to use in the engines. I have read about new kinds of airplanes in the newspapers."

"They want airplanes that will go higher, too," Jack said. "It is interesting to think that men have found ways to keep wood and metal in the air for they are heavier than air. Almost every day someone invents something to make travel in the air faster and safer."

"I want to collect pictures of all the kinds of airplanes I can," Dave said. "Then I am going to find out where airplanes can take me."

"You could go anywhere on the earth, I think," Susan said. "Airplanes go over the North Pole and over the highest mountains. They cross oceans and deserts, too."

"I will show you my book when I have finished it," Dave said. "I will put maps of the world in it. I wish we could make a trip to an airport. I would be able to get some maps there, I know."

"We can take a trip to the airport to learn more about flying," said Miss Hall.

They all decided that they would go to the airport.

Ships and Automobiles

After the trip to the airport, Harry said, "I think the bus we used in going to the airport was as interesting as the airplanes we saw. I am more interested in all kinds of automobiles than in airplanes. I use them more."

"Automobiles used to be called horseless carriages," Jack said. "That tells something about their invention. As soon as men of long ago found out that a wheel would make work easier, the way was open for the making of a cart. As soon as a cart was made, the way was open for improvements on it. Carts may have two wheels. They may have four wheels."

"Our baby cart has three wheels," Kate said.

"Carts may have any number of wheels, I suppose," Jack said.

"A wagon is only a different kind of cart," Tom said. "It is an improved kind of cart. So are carriages improved carts."

"Men may pull carts," Mary said. "So may oxen or horses. Even dogs may pull carts. Many animals work for men."

"A horseless carriage is a cart on wheels," Sam said. "Our car is a great improvement over an old two-wheeled cart, but it uses wheels just the same. It has a place for people to sit in it just as a cart has. It can carry loads just as a cart can."

"It is different from a two-wheeled cart that is drawn by one animal," Susan said.

"An engine turns the wheels," Sam said. "That is the big difference."

"The invention of an engine that could use gasoline for fuel is what made the horseless carriage possible," Jack said. "As soon as an engine was made, the way was open for inventions to use it in doing work. Traveling is work, even if it is also fun. It takes power to move anything, and if you go fast it takes more power."

"Automobiles were sometimes made with steam engines in them," Miss Hall said. "Sometimes they were made with electric motors in them. Gasoline, steam, and electricity are all used to make engines work for human beings."

"The seashore is the place to see all the ways of travel there are," Harry said. "I have seen people walking and running along the sand of the seashore. I have seen them swimming in the water. I have seen cars going along the highway near the seashore. I have seen airplanes high in the air or low over the water. Sometimes I have seen people riding horses, and where I go to the seashore some of the farmers near by bring fruits and vegetables to the market in wagons. People come and go in trains, buses, and automobiles."

"You have left out the way of travel that you can see most often at the seashore," Mary said.

"I was getting ready to name boats and ships," Harry said. "I have seen sailboats and rowboats. I have seen big ships and little ships of all kinds."

"We know what makes sailboats move," Tom said. "Wind is air in motion. Air pushes against every surface in any direction. If air is moving, it pushes with greater force. Sails are surfaces made larger to catch the wind. They are fastened to the boat, and as the wind moves them, they pull the boat through the water."

"We know what makes rowboats move," one of the girls in the class said. "A simple machine does. The oar is a lever. The oar goes through a holder on the side of the boat. It is put into the water. Then someone in the boat pushes, and the boat moves forward."

These are pictures that the boys and girls made to show all the different inventions that made sailboats and rowboats better as ways for travel.

CANOE WITH MAT SAILS

VIKING SHIP

SAILBOAT

RACING SLOOP

DUGOUT

CANOE

ROWBOAT

RACING SHELL

"The shape of a boat is an invention," Jack said. "We know that a boat is made hollow with sides so that it will take up more room in the water. Boats are made of wood and metal. If the metal in a boat should be made flat and laid on water, it would sink. If it is put together in a hollow form and laid on the water, it pushes aside as much water as it weighs.

"If it takes up more space than the amount of water it will push aside, it will float. If it takes up less space than the amount of water it will push aside, it will sink.

"We have performed experiments to show these facts. I can show you where to find the experiments in one of our books. You can do them for yourself to prove whether I am telling you facts of science."

"At the seashore or wherever there are boats on water, you can see that as more people get into a boat the boat sinks down into the water," Jane said. "If the sides of a boat are just at the surface of the water, the boat and the load in it will weigh exactly as much as the water that has been pushed aside. If even a tiny bit more weight is put into the boat, it will sink."

"Many small boats along the shore now use sails or oars," one of the boys said. "The Indians used paddles to move their canoes through the water. Large ships have engines to make them move now. There are many kinds of ships run by engines today."

"The first boats that had engines in them were made to move by paddle wheels. The engines made the paddle wheels turn in the water," Jane said. "They were called side-wheelers if the wheels were on the sides of the boat. They were called stern-wheelers if the wheels were at the back end or stern of the boat."

"The engine makes a rod turn around. The rod goes to the wheel. The wheel turns around and around in the water," Jack said. "Who could ever think of all the inventions that have been made to improve travel on ships?"

"We have left out one that I can think of," Mary said. "It is a gasoline engine to put on a rowboat to take the place of oars. The engine is not heavy. It uses gasoline from a small tank that is fastened to the engine. The engine turns a rod that has a propeller on the end. When the propeller is turned by the engine, it pushes against the water and away we go."

"Great ships that cross the ocean now use propellers like that," Miss Hall said. "Those propellers are turned by turbines. A turbine is a kind of engine. The propellers are connected with the turbines through gears. They push against the water and make the ship move forward."

"We could make some small boats like side-wheelers and stern-wheelers," Harry said. "We probably could not make them run, but we could set them on water and see what they look like."

"We could collect pictures of boats that are run by engines and propellers. Then we would have an exhibit of ships that are made to go by the use of wheels turning in water," Mary said. "I should like to help work on it. Even if we cannot make the inventions, we can see how they make ways of travel better."

This is the exhibit they made.

SIDE WHEELER

STERN WHEELER

TUGBOAT

Making Ways of Travel Safe

"Our School Safety Patrol has sent around some suggestions to help us to be careful," Miss Hall said one morning.

"May I read them to the class, Miss Hall?" Tom asked. This is what Tom read.

"Be careful when you cross streets or roads. Look both ways and do not cross when cars are coming. If there are Stop and Go signs, look at them before you start to cross. The sign will turn green by itself. You cannot hurry it. If anyone from the Safety Patrol is at the crossing, watch for his signs."

"If you must walk along a road, keep to the left, You will meet cars that are coming toward you if you do, and you can keep out of the way. If you ride a bicycle along a road, keep to the right. Ride on the same side with the cars.

"If you walk or ride on a bicycle along a road at night, carry a light and wear something white so you can be seen by others.

"Never run across a road or street in front of a car. All cars have brakes on 'them, but no car can stop at once."

"Accidents on highways happen often," Sam said. "I think we should all be careful to prevent them. If we would think about signs and suggestions such as the Safety Patrol has sent around, we would have fewer accidents."

"If we would use the safety inventions that have been made for all means of traveling, we would have fewer accidents," Mary said. "My bicycle has a brake on it. If I am not going too fast, the brake makes friction between the surface of the road and my bicycle tire. That will stop my bicycle in plenty of time."

"Automobiles have brakes for stopping in plenty of time if they are not going too fast," Jane said. "Going too fast is one cause of accidents that anyone could prevent. Anyone can go more slowly."

"Stop and Go signs are good inventions," Sam said. "If people would watch them, many accidents could be prevented."

"I have read some directions about making a small traffic light," Harry said. "If we made it, we could send it around to all the rooms in our school. We could tell how we made it and that might cause the other boys and girls to think more about traffic lights."

"We can learn more about the uses of electricity if we make the traffic light," Jack said. "I want to know as much as I can about electricity and magnets."

"The directions I read about making the small traffic light suggested that we make an electric switch, too," Harry said. "We have an electric switch in our Science Corner, but I would like to have one to use for changing our Stop and Go traffic light."

"Do we have everything we need, Harry?" Miss Hall asked.

"We need a tin can and a small punch to make holes," Harry said. "We need something to cut the tin and I can bring it from home. We need three small flashlight bulbs. We can paint clear glass the color we want. We have the cardboard and the insulated wire. We have the nails and the block of wood. We also need three Christmas tree light sockets and the bulbs."

"I can bring them to school," said Jack. "We have an old set, that we do not use, at home."

They all talked about whether to make the switch and the electric traffic light. They decided to do it. Here is the way to do both jobs.

Making a Three-Way Switch

Cut a strip of metal, about four inches long and one-half inch wide, from a tin can. Then cut from the tin can three small squares one-half inch each way. Punch a hole in one end of the metal strip. Scrape the insulation from the end of a short piece of insulated wire. Push a nail through the hole in the metal strip. Wrap the scraped end of the wire about the nail. Nail the end of the strip to a block of wood. Punch a hole in each of the metal squares. Scrape the insulation from the end of a short piece of insulated wire. Push a nail through the hole in each metal square. Wrap the scraped end of the wire about the nails. Nail the squares of metal to the block of wood. One should be just to the right, one to the left, and one beneath the metal strip already in place. To close the switch, press the strip down and slide it under the edge of one of the metal squares. To open the switch, slide the metal strip from under the metal square.

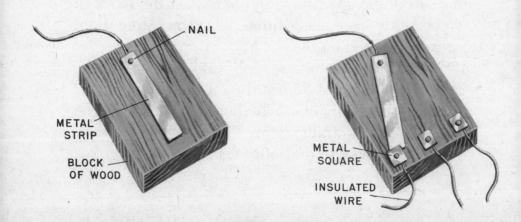

NAIL

METAL STRIP

BLOCK OF WOOD

METAL SQUARE

INSULATED WIRE

Making a Small Traffic Light

Cut a strip of heavy cardboard four inches wide and six inches long.

From a string of Christmas tree lights, cut three small sockets so that each socket has several inches of insulated wire.

Cut three holes in the cardboard large enough to receive the small end of the socket. Push the sockets tight into the holes. Screw a flashlight bulb into each socket. The drawing below shows how to do it.

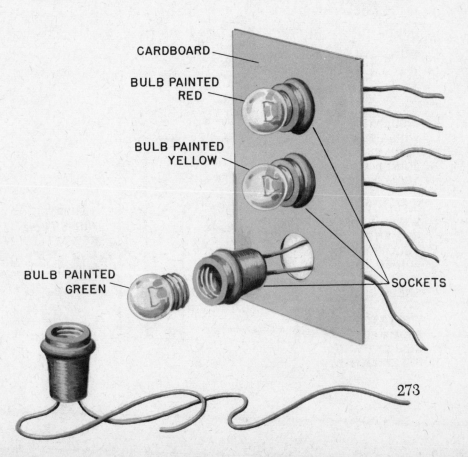

CARDBOARD

BULB PAINTED RED

BULB PAINTED YELLOW

BULB PAINTED GREEN

SOCKETS

On the back of the cardboard there will be two insulated wires from each of the small sockets. Scrape the insulation from the ends of each of the wires and join them as the drawing on this page shows.

Colored cellophane may be fastened over the flashlight bulbs or they may be covered with thin paint. One bulb should be red, one yellow, and one green.

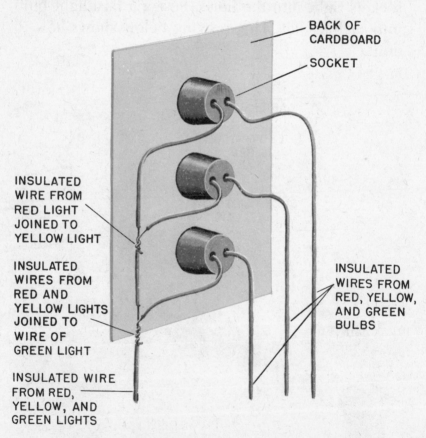

BACK OF CARDBOARD

SOCKET

INSULATED WIRE FROM RED LIGHT JOINED TO YELLOW LIGHT

INSULATED WIRES FROM RED AND YELLOW LIGHTS JOINED TO WIRE OF GREEN LIGHT

INSULATED WIRE FROM RED, YELLOW, AND GREEN LIGHTS

INSULATED WIRES FROM RED, YELLOW, AND GREEN BULBS

You are now ready to connect the traffic light to the switch and a dry cell. If the wires on the switch and the traffic light are not long enough to make the connections, scrape off the insulation and add a piece of insulated wire of the length you need.

The drawing on this page shows how to connect the traffic light to the switch and the dry cell.

When the connection is made, the traffic light is ready to be put to work.

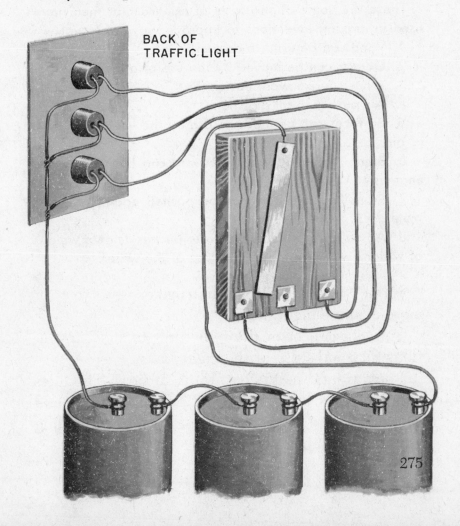

BACK OF
TRAFFIC LIGHT

What We Know about Inventions and Ways of Travel

The small traffic light and the homemade switch were taken to all the rooms. When the questions that others asked had all been answered, Miss Hall showed a chart she had made.

FACTS USED TO IMPROVE TRAVEL

These are some of the facts of science that men have used in making inventions to improve ways of travel.

1. Wind can be used to do work.
2. Objects can be moved by the use of a lever.
3. Wheels make work easier.
4. Air pushes in all directions.
5. Surfaces can be made to rise by the use of the push of air.
6. Steam, gasoline, and electricity can be used to run engines.
7. Propellers and oars can be pushed against air and water.
8. An object that floats on water pushes its own weight of water away and takes the place of the water.

Name some inventions that make use of one or more of these eight facts.

You can collect or draw pictures to show inventions that make use of the eight facts.

Look around in any car, train, or boat. The facts that scientists have found out by observation and experiment are being put to use to make traveling more comfortable.

276

Using Science

Wherever you are, at school or at home, inventions can be seen that make use of what scientists have found out. Sometimes an inventor is the one who found out the fact of science. Sometimes the inventor uses what a scientist has found out.

Pencil sharpeners, ink bottles, globes, rocking chairs, fountain pens, typewriters, and all objects in common use in schools and homes are inventions that make use of some facts of science.

Windows have clear glass in them. Scientists found out how to make glass clear. They also found how to make steel springs from iron that was in the earth. Springs are used in chairs and beds.

Scientists found out about electric currents in wires. Then they found out how to turn the current off. Lights can be turned on or off by an electric switch.

Most people simply use objects of all kinds and do not think about how they came to be made. Anyone who takes a trip is interested first of all in taking the trip safely and quickly. He is not often interested in all the inventions that have been put together to make an automobile or an airplane.

Wheels, speedometers, temperature gauges, oil gauges, brakes, cushions, side mirror, headlights, engines, and a hundred other inventions are put together to make modern ways of travel. Look around and observe them.

Science Words

air pressure—the push of air on a surface
antenna—a feeler on the head of an insect
artificial—made by man
astronomer—a scientist who studies the stars and the sky

bacteria—one-celled plants seen only through a microscope
balanced diet—foods that should be eaten for growth,
    energy, and health
barometer—an instrument for measuring air pressure

candle power—the brightness of a light as compared with
    the light of a candle of a special size
carbon dioxide—a gas made of carbon and oxygen
cell—the unit that makes up plant and animal bodies
chemical—the material that makes or may be combined to
    make the molecules of substance
chlorine—a chemical often used in making water safe to
    drink
climate—the usual kind of weather that any place has over
    long stretches of time
compressed—made to fit into a smaller space
constellation—a group of stars that seem placed to make
    a picture in the sky

disease germs—very small plants and animals that cause
    sickness

electric current—a flow of electricity in a circuit
electric fuse—an invention to cut off the current when too
    much electricity is flowing in a wire
erosion—the wearing away of soil

fulcrum—the part of a lever that does not move

geologist—a scientist who studies the earth
gravity—the pull of the earth on other substances

278

humus—decaying plants and animals in soil

light meter—an instrument used to measure the brightness
of light

mammal—that kind of animal of which the mother gives
milk for its babies
mold—a woolly-like plant which grows on other plant and
animal products
molecule—the smallest part of a substance that is still the
substance

natural—made by nature
nitrogen—a chemical that is part of the air and of many
other substances

pasteurized—heated to about 140 degrees Fahrenheit and
kept in airtight containers
planet—a large heavenly body that revolves around the sun
pollen—the dusty-looking powder in a flower that helps the
plant produce seeds
protein—the substance found in lean meat, cheese, eggs,
and beans that helps the growth of animal bodies

rain gauge—an instrument for measuring the amount of
rainfall
revolves—to go around anything
rotate—to spin like a top, or to turn on an axis

short circuit—a short path that an electric current may
follow
substance—anything made of chemicals

terrarium—a small place where land animals and plants
live
thermometer—an instrument to measure temperature

wind gauge—an instrument for measuring wind speed

List of Experiments

Index